*8 toughest
problems
parents face
and how to
handle them*

To Billy & Annie,

To one of my best
H.S. friends and
his wife. I hope
you enjoy this.

Fondly,
Chuck

8 toughest problems parents face and how to handle them

Kent R. Brand, A.C.S.W.
D. Charles Williams, Ph.D.

Tyndale House Publishers, Inc.,
Wheaton, Illinois

Unless otherwise identified, all Scripture
quotations are from *The Holy Bible,* New
International Version, copyright 1978, 1984 by the
New York International Bible Society. Used by
permission of Zondervan Bible Publishers.

Previously published under the title *Strategies for
Children* by Kent Brand and Chuck Williams,
Rt. 2, Box 24, Newberry, FL 32669.

First Tyndale House printing, May 1989
Library of Congress Catalog Card Number 88-51926
ISBN 0-8423-0756-7

To Joel, Jenny, Jamie, and Jessica, out of my deep love and affection.

To my beautiful wife, Becky, who has helped me immensely in planning strategies for our children.

To my parents, Roy and Eula Brand, who also deserve premiere status because of their strategy to lead me to Christ and a maturing faith.

To my secretary, Paula Levine, who has worked tirelessly and efficiently through countless unexpected barriers in the completion of this book.

To Olive Scott and members of my Christian Family Services staff and home fellowship group for their help in preparing the final manuscripts.

To Toney C. Mulhollan, our printer, with special thanks for his tremendous hard work, sacrifice, and love for God.

—Kent R. Brand

To two very loved boys, Christopher and David, who have inspired a great deal of the anecdotes and lessons herein.

To my wife and their mother. Her astute insight and attentiveness has always amazed me.

To my parents, Robert L. and Betty J. Williams, and my in-laws, Walter and Jacqueline Lastition, who did an excellent job as parents on their own children. My heartfelt love and gratitude goes to each of these very precious people in my life.

—D. Charles Williams

Chapter 3 Dedicated to my father, whom I have grown to love and respect with each passing year.—D. Charles Williams

Chapter 5 Dedicated to my four children, who are the apple of my eye.—Kent R. Brand

Contents

Introduction

This book is different. It may surprise you with its practicality because it presents a very innovative approach to
child-rearing and parenting. It attempts to blend the two
seemingly opposite philosophies of Christianity and
psychology into a common-sense approach that really
works. Our intentions have been to take everyday problems
of family living and development and apply Christian principles of faith, hope, and love with effective techniques
used in the field of counseling. In many Christian books
there appears to be very little acknowledgment of
psychological principles. Likewise in psychology, there is
almost an absence of credit given to the Christian influence
many counseling concepts possess. Our efforts have been
to extract from each those things that work, giving our
readers both principles and practicality.

If you are a parent who has wondered what to do or
how to handle specific problems in your family in an effective Christian manner, this book might help you.

This book has been the result of more than two years of
work and twenty-five years of combined clinical counseling
experience with literally hundreds of families. It hardly

answers all the problems parents face with their children. It does, however, try to use common sense, creative strategies, psychological techniques, and, most of all, spiritual insight from a Christian perspective to make the process of growing up as a parent or a child a smooth, healthy, and fun experience.

D. Charles Williams, Ph.D.
Licensed Applied Psychologist

Kent R. Brand, M.S.W., A.C.S.W.
Licensed Clinical Social Worker

About the Authors

Kent R. Brand

Kent is a social worker for Christian Family Services, Inc., in Gainesville, Florida. He received an Associate of Arts degree in Bible from York College in 1967, a Bachelor of Arts degree in Bible from Harding College in 1969, and a Master of Social Work degree from the University of North Carolina in 1974. Kent is a man who has continued to seek excellence in his counseling and fathering skills. His eighteen years of experience in marriage and thirteen years of experience in counseling certainly qualify him to give strategies that work for parents in need of help. He is a member of the Academy of Certified Social Workers and is a licensed social worker in Florida. More important, he is a man of prayer, Bible study, and fervent evangelism.

D. Charles Williams

Charles is a psychologist in private practice in Atlanta, Georgia. He received his Baccaleureate in Psychology from Clemson University and his Doctorate in Counseling from the University of Florida. Dr. Williams has received extensive marriage and family therapy training and has been in active clinical practice for more than thirteen years. He has directed and supervised psychiatric programs, mental health clinics, and graduate counseling students. His list of memberships in national associations includes the American Association for Marriage and Family Therapy, the American Psychological Association, the Georgia Psychological Association, and the American Society of Clinical Hypnosis. He is a dedicated husband, father, and Christian who is committed to serving God, his family, and mankind.

Samuel D. Laing

Sam serves as an evangelist in Miami, Florida. Prior to that he was in the ministry as an evangelist in Atlanta, Georgia, for a number of years. Sam graduated from the University of Florida in 1971. He served as a campus minister for Crossroads Church of Christ for more than ten years. He is known for his wisdom, depth, and insight into the human heart. Besides having an exemplary family life, he is effective in communicating principles for practical family living. He and his lovely wife, Geri, have been married for fifteen years, and have four children, Elizabeth, David, Jonathan, and Alexandra.

Elizabeth Carter Alvarez

Elizabeth was born on February 16, 1964, in Searcy, Arkansas. She is the oldest of four children and has attended the Church of Christ all of her life. She became a Christian on April 26, 1978, at Sandy Springs Church of Christ in Atlanta, Georgia. She was faithful until the age of seventeen when for a brief time she left the Lord and got involved with drugs and alcohol. Elizabeth went through the Straight, Inc. program in Atlanta in 1982–1983. Upon graduation in 1983, she became committed to helping families with the same problems her family had experienced. She searched out scripturally the concept she had learned in the Straight, Inc. program. She is an English major and hopes to have a career in Christian writing. She works full time at present and is pursuing a degree at Georgia State University in 1988. In 1987 she was married to David Alvarez.

1
Building Self-Esteem in Our Children
D. Charles Williams, Ph.D.

FINDING THE JEWELS

Each of us, young or old, is special and unique. No one has our particular combination of characteristics. Only we have our smile, our sense of humor, our walk. Although we are all somewhat similar in the way we look, think, and the common needs we have, no one is just like us, just as no two snowflakes are exactly the same. Recognizing our uniqueness should help us to realize our inherent individual value.

We often spend too much time comparing ourselves with others and the qualities they possess. Each of us must learn to have a sense of self-worth and then enjoy being ourselves. Kids need to like who they are. Children and adults often ask themselves, "Who am I?" Each of us is a combination of various roles, such as male, female, son, daughter, husband, wife, employee, employer, or neighbor. Our view of ourselves in these roles contributes to our definition of who we are.

Do you ever wonder why self-doubt is so prevalent in our society? These feelings of inferiority are often fostered in the first five or six years of life, though they may not actually show up until adolescent years. Rather than accepting each other for our own unique qualities, we tend to scrutinize others for their weaknesses and reward only those who have a great deal of intelligence, attractiveness, talent, athletic ability, or money. By doing so, are we subtly implying that all other qualities are less valuable than these?

Someone once said, "All people are equal, but some are more equal than others." As parents, it is our job not to allow this way of thinking to influence the way we treat our children. Each child is a bundle of possibilities just waiting to be discovered, developed, and celebrated. By giving our children the opportunity to pursue those interests that they see as important, we communicate a sense of value and acceptance for who they are.

In my office, I often hear children and adults say, "People wouldn't like me if they knew the real me." This message is unintentional but subtly reinforced by significant others who try to mold that individual to their own expectations. As parents, we run the risk of making a big mistake if we attempt to guide our children into following after our past dreams and aspirations. In the short run, it may be less interesting for us to encourage our children to pursue those areas in which they have a personal interest. In the long run, they will benefit more from this, and we will be happier for them.

I have always appreciated my parents for letting me pursue my music in high school and college, even though I knew my dad would have preferred my playing football. My musical skills still are an enjoyment to me almost twenty years later. As an aside, I did win a football trophy for the "best running-back" in the league for the several years I did play.

A CHILD'S TWO BASIC EMOTIONAL NEEDS

Children value themselves to the degree that they feel valued by significant others.

Children have two basic emotional needs. The first is for the feeling that "I am loved." The second is for the feeling that "I am worthwhile." These two needs are the basic elements in the development of a child's self-esteem.

If a child feels inherently valuable because he exists, apart from anything he does, he will feel important and loved. Paul told the Corinthians: "You have such a place in our hearts that we would live and die with you. I have great confidence in you; I take great pride in you. I am greatly encouraged; in all our troubles, my joy knows no bounds" (2 Cor. 7:4).

A sincere expression of genuine feelings, like Paul's, would help anyone feel affirmed and important. We communicate such messages in many ways during the day by the patience we use with our children, the tone of our voices, the time we take to answer their questions, the interest we show in spite of their many interruptions, and our belief in their ability to master activities in which they are involved.

We teach our children that they are worthwhile by helping them learn to handle themselves, in their environment, with confidence. It is easy to underestimate the value of helping a child learn to do something himself. It requires our time and patience as well as our allowing them to do it on their own, making the mistakes that are necessary to learn from experience. Even though the time that it takes in the initial stages of learning something may seem costly to us, it is an investment that will save us time in the long run. It will also help them to develop confidence in themselves and satisfaction in their abilities. It is an invaluable gift for a child to know that he has something to offer others, and that he does it well. There are no shortcuts. Self-esteem is no accident. From parents, self-esteem for their children takes a heavy investment of time, patience, practice, and praise.

SHAPING THE INNER ARMOR
OF EMOTIONAL STRENGTH

Have you ever wondered why some children are more emotionally resilient than others? Why do some children who experience early loss, deprivation, trauma, and abuse seem to spring back and thrive in spite of the painful past?

Recent research has begun to show which characteristics in a family foster invulnerability within children toward stressful circumstances. At least six factors help young children develop this inner armor against future affronts to their self-esteem. The first is *positive emotional tone.*

Positive emotional tone refers to the atmosphere in which a child lives. For instance, if there is a lot of positive energy, such as smiling or speaking cheerfully among the parents and children in the home, a sense of well-being and security can easily be established. This emotional atmosphere lets a child know that life is safe and happy around him.

A second important factor that develops a child's inner emotional armor is *responsivity,* which refers to the parents' reacting to a child's needs and his attempts to get attention. When a child gets almost immediate response to his needs, he feels cared for and significant. Of course, in older children, these attempts to get attention can develop into constant, discourteous interruptions and must be controlled. For younger children, though, it is an essential way to let them know they count.

The third factor is *comforting.* The amount of physical comforting a child receives has a great influence on how secure and loved he feels. Comforting involves the amount of holding, cuddling, playing, and reassuring a child receives, both physically and verbally, from a parent. *Comforting* does not simply refer to picking up the child every time he cries, which could actually undermine self-esteem.

The fourth factor is *anticipating.* Parents who are thoughtful enough to anticipate the things that will please their child, or protect him from what might scare him, show the child that his needs are understood. When one of my sons was younger, he was afraid of dogs because of an early incident in which he was bitten in the face. When one of the neighbor's large pets would venture into the yard, we would use that opportunity to intercept and gradually introduce him to this unexpected event. By controlling his amount of exposure to the animals, we could assure the experience would be a positive one. He was fortunately able to gradually get over his fearful reaction. Our anticipation of his reaction provided a security that enabled him to face his fear constructively. Anticipation also involves preparing a child's favorite food or presenting him with a treat he likes. It simply means offering the same thoughtfulness and courtesy that we show our friends.

Another important factor is *stimulation*. Effective parents are able to provide new and interesting experiences for their children. New toys, games, places, or experiences can give invaluable enrichment to our children. Exposing them to all kinds of opportunities is one way of increasing their intelligence and expanding their interests in life.

The final factor is called *coordination*. This refers to the synchrony between parent and child that allows them to interact together as a family unit. An example of this is a child stretching out his hands to a parent, who picks him up. It also involves a child reaching back to receive something an adult is handing him. These types of coordinated interactions subtly define an inherent relationship between parent and child. It is a nonverbal form of communication that implies attention, involvement, and acceptance between adult and child. These six factors combine to create a security within a child that says, "I am important," "I matter," "Life is safe and secure," and "I am cared for."

TRANSITIONS

Similar to adults, children experience various transitions in life. Since we have had the opportunity to experience these transitions, our experience often helps us to give a child adequate preparation for the different phases of his or her life. For instance, it is important for a child to have a positive first experience when introduced to something new in his life. Such experiences—the first day of nursery school, kindergarten, first grade, junior high, high school, or tryouts for a play or team—pose a number of threats to a child's self-esteem. It is always helpful for adults to be involved with their children during these transitions. Such involvement might include discussing what to expect, accompanying him on that first day, and later exploring how that experience went. Sharing our own personal anecdotes can be very enlightening to our children as they face their new frontiers.

A number of significant events were indelibly etched in my mind when I was a child. I recall on the first day of elementary school being attacked by a second grader. Fortunately, my father had taught me how to defend myself, and this second grader was embarrassed in front of his friends. During that same age period, on the first day of baseball tryouts, I recall running out on the field asking my peers to throw me the ball. When one of them did, to my embarrassment, it hit me right between the eyes. Fortunately, my father was there to talk about this situation or else I might have held back indefinitely.

In eighth grade, when my family moved from one state to another, I began in a new school. On the first day of this transfer, the teacher unfortunately bragged to the class about my good grades. At recess, I found myself in the middle of a fight.

On the first day of football tryouts in high school, I received a serious back injury, and the line coach seemed unconcerned. In fact, he made derogatory comments instead of trying to recognize that a young man's self-esteem was hanging in the balance.

These are but a few of the typical transitions in a child's life during which time an attentive and understanding adult can be very helpful. Anticipating the potential problems these transitions can cause, and effectively preparing a child for them, can mean the difference between success and failure, motivation and defeat, low and high self-esteem.

TWO IMPORTANT TIMES OF THE DAY

In our busy society, we often miss opportunities to "check in" with each other during the day. Two of the most important times of the day for input with our children are early in the morning and late in the evening. Our first encounter with our child sets the tone for the day. If this is positive, encouraging, and meaningful, the rest of the day can be a success for them. Before bedtime, interaction with our children permits us to discuss the events of the day.

Children often do not disclose on cue and need opportunities to express their thoughts and feelings to an attentive parent. If a child knows there will be time to talk, they will be more inclined to make use of those times. It also provides an excellent opportunity to generate "food for thought" for our children, and develop a positive attitude upon which to end the day.

ELIMINATING CRITICAL INFLUENCES

Negativism and criticism from within or from without are perhaps the most destructive forces that work on a young person's self-esteem. Our society is geared toward being the best, so we feel we cannot make mistakes. This unrealistic view causes us to place on ourselves virtually impossible expectations. Because of these pressures, students often make disqualifying statements about their abilities such as, "I'm just an average student," or "I never do well on tests." Occasionally an individual will try something new but sabotage his performance by saying something like, "Oh, I'll never do this." An obese person's fatalistic attitude becomes obvious when he sits down to a meal and says, "Everything I eat turns to fat."

Parents may even create a self-fulfilling prophecy by telling their children not to spill the milk. We are constantly barraged with negative influences from the newspaper and the television. Even many current musical lyrics advocate no hope. One current song states, "You are defective; why not try suicide?"

Because of the destructive influence of criticism in families, one prominent author has established what he calls a "no-knock" policy in his home. This means that no one is allowed to put themselves or others down in their home. It is important that as parents we discourage our children from complaining, and especially blaming others. We, ourselves, can avoid using derogatory names in teasing our children. Names such as "Shorty," "Klutz," "Chubby," or "Buns," only reinforce a child's perceived flaws. Paul encouraged us not to let any unwholesome talk come out of our mouths, but only what is helpful for building others up according to their needs, that it may benefit those who listen (Eph. 4:29). Often these pet names cause our children to focus more on external characteristics than is healthy.

If we reduce the emphasis on external measures of success, they may more clearly see the importance of their internal qualities. Of course, we should be aware of the premium that young people place on physical appearance and help them reach their goals of looking the best that they can; yet, other strengths can be accentuated and encouraged much more.

SHAME-PROOFING OUR CHILDREN

As parents, we are in an advantageous position to teach our children how to handle setbacks without fearing criticism or looking foolish. If we are able to laugh at our mistakes without defending ourselves, our children will do the same. Giving ourselves permission to look foolish may be one of the most liberating things we can ever do. Of course, appearing foolish is associated with being vulnerable, which goes against our "need to be perfect" image in society. Admitting we do not know it all, however, is the first step to learning something. This allows us to be human and removes our need to be perfect. Words like, "I'm afraid," "I need help," or "I made a mistake," usually break the barriers down between us and others.

Sociological research has taught us that a speaker's credibility is heightened if he demonstrates or shares shortcomings about himself to his audience. His openness allows people to see him as a normal person just like themselves, and enables them to better relate to his message.

If we teach our children to own up to what they perceive to be their own inadequacies without belittling themselves, they can more aptly learn to accept and use constructive criticism from others. Using humor that addresses the situation, pointing out what is funny, keeps us from negatively accusing ourselves personally. We can shame-proof ourselves and our children by telling them, "It is okay," "So you blew it," and "It did look silly, but you're a good person and it's okay," "People care about you anyway for yourself and not just for what you do." By sharing these experiences with friends, we remove the stigma of embarrassments in our own minds. Often to our surprise, openness causes us to realize that most people have made the same mistakes.

TEACHING HOPE AND PERSEVERANCE

One summer when I was a teenager in Greenville, South Carolina, several of my best friends and I spent a great deal of time swimming at a local pool. Two of those friends, Mike and Steve, were excellent divers. Their graceful acrobatics on the diving board made me envious of them, so I decided to also learn to do flips and twists off the high board. After several bellyflops and backburners, I was not as enthusiastic about the idea. Nevertheless, I knew that they had only become as good as they were through trial and error. Determined not to be a quitter, I continued the painful process of learning how to dive. We have the opportunity to learn this lesson of hope and perseverance time and time again, but it takes some risks on our part.

As parents, we are in a position to develop hope in our children by our faith in God that all things do work out. Our example of faith in facing life's many ups and downs will be more of a lesson than anything we could say. My mother is perhaps one of the best examples of hope that I observed as a child. She was an eternal optimist who knew that somehow God would work out each situation even if she had no clue about how it might occur.

In a child's life, the existence of one caring adult can make a big difference. Perhaps this is why my favorite scripture is: "And we know that in all things God works for the good of those who love him, who have been called according to his purpose" (Rom. 8:28). Hope also involves less emphasis on what the future holds and more on who holds the future. In our rather compulsive society, we are overplanned and organized in such detail that our security is imposed by the control we maintain of our lives. This approach to life fosters a sense of self-sufficiency that causes us to need God and others less. This is one reason why there has been such an increase in the 1980s of work-aholism, anxiety attacks, addictive behavior, phobias, and rigid compulsiveness. When we have no one to rely on but ourselves, life can be a very terrifying place to live. Paul wrote, " 'My power is made perfect in weakness.' Therefore I will boast all the more gladly in my weaknesses. . . . For when I am weak, then I am strong" (2 Cor. 12:9-10). Our recognition of our own shortcomings and the acknowledgment of Christ's all-sustaining power allows us to rely on him for the future. This is an invaluable lesson to teach our children, and yet one they will only learn by our example.

LIFE IS DIFFICULT

Many of us believe this statement, but we don't like it and wish it could be different. Our lives today are often geared toward making life easier and more comfortable for ourselves. When we reflect back upon our lives, it was the difficulties we faced that have caused each of us to develop stamina, character, and perseverance. As I have mentioned before, my father is perhaps the best example of dogged determination to whom I was exposed as a child. His persistence in a project helped me recognize the importance of "hanging in there" until a solution was discovered.

Our children are often inundated by the philosophy that those who look the best, are the smartest, have the most money, and possess natural talent will succeed in life.

If we allow the media to indoctrinate our children with this mentality, we will assure them of discouragement in their lives. When I was in my first two years at Clemson University, I was flunking out. Even though I was studying and working as hard as I thought I could, I was not making the grades, so I dropped out for a year. I was secretly afraid that I did not have the intelligence to succeed in college. When I did return, I met a beautiful young freshman who took her studies seriously. She not only worked hard, but she "worked smart." She planned her work and worked her plan. As a psychology student, I had a great volume of reading to do. As a nursing student, she had not only a great volume of material to read, but she also had to memorize, integrate, and apply empirical information. As my interest in her grew, I realized that if I wanted to spend time with her, I would have to study.

This tenacious young woman taught me the lesson that perseverance meant doing whatever it took (no matter how hard or how long) to accomplish the goal. She taught me that lesson so effectively that I used it to convince her to marry me. I have remembered her invaluable example many times since I received my doctorate in counseling.

By the mile it's a trial, but by the inch it's a cinch.

We can teach our children that they can do anything God expects of them if they trust him, work hard, and persevere. By starting out with small goals that our children are assured of achieving, they can begin with success. There is, of course, no substitute for rehearsing and practicing many, many, many times. My oldest son, Christopher, is currently taking karate. He is now working on his third belt and has shown improvement steadily. The beauty of these programs for children is that they begin on a very small scale. As the children learn the routines, they are rewarded with stripes and belts. No child is allowed to test for the next belt unless the instructors know they can pass. This is not to say that children should never experience failure; yet it is important that they experience success in the beginning so that they can develop a sense of competence and confidence. This motivates us all to try harder.

When a child is reluctant to try something new for fear of failing, he or she can often be encouraged to attempt it by observing a friend who is learning or has mastered that activity. When we were trying to get Christopher to learn how to swim, hold his breath, and put his face in the water, we had to solicit the services of his little friend, Travis, to show him how easy this task was. Upon seeing Travis jump into the water with reckless abandon, Christopher followed suit. This was also helpful when Christopher's younger brother, David, began to venture into the water. Seeing his big brother's lack of fear gave him the confidence to try it on his own.

An additional technique for helping our children believe more in what God can do through them is that of imagining success. We have all seen others riding down the road singing and moving their head to a song on the radio as if they were on stage. This "armchair participation" helps us imagine ourselves as succeeding in a particular endeavor. We can also teach our children to visualize themselves succeeding. If we can see it completed in our own mind before we actually attempt an activity, we can anticipate and emotionally prepare for the task at hand. We have all probably found ourselves talking through an ensuing conversation or upcoming presentation to prepare ourselves for the event. By encouraging our children to walk through the activity in their own minds, they can prepare for each step of the way. Many sports magazines encourage us to "lock in" successful movements and techniques so that we can replay and reproduce them in real life.

If a child believes that things will work out, if he tries hard enough and persists long enough, he will succeed in those things in which he is most interested. Our belief and support of our children along the way is paramount for them to develop the building blocks needed for discipline and skill acquisition.

TREAT YOUR CHILD AS SOMEBODY SPECIAL—A WINNER

Each child needs to feel wholly accepted. He must be accepted unconditionally and not just when he does well. A child needs to feel loved and accepted no matter what happens. This self-acceptance begins early in life by touching, kissing, wrestling, and playing with our children when they are young as well as when they are older. Touch instills life and affirms value. I recently saw a coffee cup that stated, "A hug could just make my day!" I work in a group counseling practice with other counselors and psychologists who are free with their affection, not only with our clients, but with each other. You see, we know that physical touch often says more than words ever could. An affectionate, nonsexual embrace can say, "I accept you," as effectively as anything can.

We teach our children how important they are by how intently we listen to them and how important we value what they say. Complete eye contact says to a child, "What you are telling me is very important because you are very important." By allowing our children to speak for themselves instead of speaking for them, we convince them that they have something to contribute. A clue to how a child thinks of himself can often be seen in how he responds when introduced to other individuals. At those times, he is presenting himself and his opinions of himself in his body language.

It is important to teach our children how to meet others: to look directly at them, to shake hands firmly, to answer the phone appropriately, to greet friends enthusiastically, and to speak up when addressed. When we take the time to introduce our children by name in a group of people, we are saying that our child counts, that he is important, and his presence here is valued.

All children are born to win. They are winners from the beginning. There is no one like them, nor will there ever be another who has the same combination of characteristics, qualities, and potentials. There is no limit to what they can do or how creative they can be. The more we believe in them, the more they believe in themselves. This attitude was captured beautifully by Paul when he said, "You have such a place in our hearts that we would live and die with you. I have great confidence in you; I take great pride in you. I am greatly encouraged; in all our troubles, my joy knows no bounds" (2 Cor. 7:3-4). Wouldn't it be great if each of us had someone who felt this way toward us throughout our lives? Let's be that person to our children!

2

Sibling Rivalry
Kent R. Brand, A.C.S.W.

DESCRIPTION OF THE PROBLEM

Perhaps the question most often asked by parents is about how to deal with sibling rivalry. No parents are exempt from the inevitability of it—not even the experts. In years past, my children battled over the seating arrangement in our automobile, and with a family of four children in a small station wagon, this became an interesting issue. The most prestigious seat was always the front middle seat between both parents. I remember vacations when my wife and I dreaded a long twelve-hour trip because we knew how the children would react to one another.

No matter how strong the marriage, or how committed the parents are to the children, sibling rivalry will always be a reality. Even the most cooperative families must deal with it. A few of the issues that children choose to fight over will be chores, TV programs, hurt feelings, and treatment. Sometimes what one child considers "kidding around" will seem obnoxious to another child, and fights develop. This is not to say that parents must throw up their hands and declare the situation hopeless. I believe that with well-planned interaction, sibling rivalry can be minimized.

Recently, my heart was warmed to hear of an incident

between my six-year-old son and two-year-old daughter. They were both playing when my daughter started crying because something was not going quite her way. At that point, my son chimed in and said, "Daddy says, blessed are the peacemakers." In that situation, peace and cooperation followed. Obviously, not all sibling rivalry can be resolved with such a simple solution, but it is encouraging to see that children can learn to love each other and play together with cooperation.

Why did God plan for most families to have siblings? Sometimes we concentrate so much on the negative aspects of sibling rivalry that we forget the great advantages of these family relationships. One obvious reason for having sibling relationships is that brothers and sisters provide the opportunity to learn cooperation. Children can learn to share by sharing toys. They learn affection from one another. A family of siblings is a great place for a child to learn how to interact with other people in problem solving. These problem-solving skills carry over to help them solve problems in adult life. It is crucial that parents begin to teach their children from an early age these problem-solving skills. Small children should hear often, "In this family, we love each other." Respect, affection, and love can be reasonably expected by the parents.

Another advantage of sibling relationships is that children learn at an early age to interact in groups. Someday these children will have to interact with others at school, college, work, and in their future families. The group atmosphere of the home will help them to develop these skills.

Children who have no siblings are somewhat unfortunate; since their children will have no aunts and uncles, their extended families will be small. It can also be a tremendous advantage for the parents, once they get old, to have had more than one child to share the responsibility of caring for them in their old age.

The bond between siblings is one of the strongest bonds on earth. The loyalty that can develop is another great advantage of sibling relationships. The Greeks had a word for love called *storge.* This kind of love is a psychological and biological bond between family members. This strong bond should be used by the parents to help the children feel special. Children can be taught that sibling relationships are precious. The loyalty they demonstrate toward each other can help a child feel he is never alone, and that he or she can always depend on brothers and sisters. Even when marital problems threaten the security of the home, sibling relationships can provide the stability necessary to enable the children to cope.

Sibling rivalry is not just a twentieth-century phenomenon. There is a long history of rivalry in sibling relationships. The first one recorded was that of Cain and Abel. Cain became jealous of Abel's sacrifice, which was considered more acceptable by God. In reaction, Cain took revenge for being outdone by killing Abel. The sibling rivalry between Jacob and Esau was actually fostered by their parents, Isaac and Rebekah, who played favorites. Their error in showing favoritism resulted in cheating, lying, and feelings of intense hatred and fear among the brothers. In fact, Jacob and Esau spent many years separated from one another because of these bad feelings.

Another example of sibling jealousy was between Joseph and his brothers. Joseph was obviously his father's favorite. His father gave a beautiful coat of many colors to him only. To make matters worse, when Joseph told about the dreams he had received from the Lord, his brothers were extremely jealous. They plotted to kill him, threw him in a well, and eventually sold him into slavery. This story had a happy ending, however. After many years of separation, Joseph, as second-in-command of Egypt, helped his brothers through a great difficulty and became reconciled with them. There was a very emotional scene of many tears. Even then, his brothers did not trust him to forgive them.

There are many other examples where, instead of reconciliation, jealous revenge was sought against siblings. In the New Testament, we have the example of a prominent ruler named Herod, who took his brother Philip's wife. Jesus also told the story of a young son who left home, squandered his inheritance, and came back home penniless. When his father started to celebrate his return, the prodigal son's older brother became angry at his father's accepting attitude and at what he thought was favoritism toward the younger brother.

Not all sibling relationships in the Bible were negative. There is the example of Andrew and Peter. Though they were very different in their personalities, they appeared quite close. Andrew was the quieter one, but after finding Jesus, brought Peter to him. Even though Peter excelled and became one of Jesus' closer friends, it did not seem to bother Andrew. They both seemed to have confidence in themselves and their love for each other. Moses and Aaron also had a positive relationship, though there was some strife between him and his sister, Miriam. Even though Moses was the younger sibling, Moses and Aaron enjoyed a very good working relationship in leading the Israelites out of Egypt. Only one instance of jealousy was recorded, and God dealt with that jealousy in a very decisive manner. From then on, Moses and Aaron had a great sibling relationship.

In conclusion, we can see that sibling relationships have always been a part of family interaction. These sibling relationships can either be positive or negative.

AGE OF OCCURRENCE

Sibling rivalry can begin even before the younger child is born and can extend all the way into adulthood if precautions and preparations are not taken within a family. If a sibling finds out that he is going to have a new brother or sister, careful communication and assurances can help minimize the initial rivalry at birth. As the youngest sibling grows and becomes more mobile, there will be a strong tendency for him to insist on having things his way, which can greatly infuriate older siblings. Sibling rivalry can become quite intense in preschool years because these children do not have the reasoning skills of an older child at this point and are naturally self-centered. Such rivalry can be difficult for elementary-age children because they do not have the reasoning powers of an adolescent. Adolescent years are difficult because children are going through tremendous emotional and physical changes. Their conscience and values are forming, and they are also beginning to try to fit in with their peers. All these factors can stimulate negative relationships with siblings.

As one can see, there are no perfect ages for handling sibling rivalry. The purpose of this chapter is to help minimize sibling rivalry and produce the respect, love, and bond that will help siblings get along in their younger years and later in their adult lives.

POSSIBLE CAUSES

Whatever the causes, the fact remains that sibling rivalry is not an illusion. It is very real. One theory suggests that birth order is a significant contributing factor. According to this theory, the family structure greatly influences the interaction of siblings. Firstborn children are naturally more outgoing and aggressive. This child, because he faces responsibilities, quickly learns adult skills and thus possesses a higher motivation to achieve. However, this child may be put in situations where he can be given too much responsibility or where he feels too much pressure to excel. This can, in turn, create a strained relationship with the siblings. They may possibly pass on the frustrations they feel from their parents toward the younger children.

Middle children sometimes have to struggle with a sense of identity. They get the "hand-me-downs" from the oldest child and many times do not get as much attention as the youngest or oldest child. Their lack of identity can cause them to want to lash out at the younger or older sibling.

The child born last typically receives a great deal of attention from older siblings and feels very secure in the relationship. However, this child may use all this attention to manipulate older siblings and parents. If the child feels resentment about being the youngest, this may also cause a strain in brother-sister relationships.[1]

A second theory regarding causal factors of sibling rivalry is the quality of the parents' relationships. This theory states that parents who are poor examples of resolving conflicts in communication will foster a high degree of sibling rivalry in children.

Perhaps these children will learn to respond based on the models with which they have become familiar. Likewise, positive examples of conflict resolution in parents cultivate constructive resolution of problems between siblings.

A third theory of sibling rivalry suggests that conflict develops from the deprivation of possessions. This theory states that sibling rivalry really stems from the wants and desires within the individual siblings. In 1975, Steinmetz found that a major source of conflict among young siblings was over possessions.[2] Felsen more specifically defined conflict as "competition for property, space, and other tangible goods that they share by virtue of their membership in the family."[3] This is illustrated in the Book of James:

> *What causes fights and quarrels among you? Don't they come from your desires that battle within you? You want something but don't get it. You kill and covet, but you cannot have what you want. You quarrel and fight. You do not have, because you do not ask God. When you ask, you do not receive, because you ask with the wrong motives, that you may spend what you get on your pleasures. (4:1-3)*

Parents who are concerned about sibling rivalry should be aware of the great value that a child places upon possessions. Many times the value of a possession can become momentarily stronger than the value of the sibling relationship.

The last theory is that of status deprivation. This occurs when the parents show favoritism toward a particular child, or their favorite changes from day to day. Such favoritism fosters insecurity, competition, and jealousy among siblings. It is important for each child to be treated equally, yet appropriately, for his age level. Children need to be taught that they are each equally important. However, they must also realize that with age comes responsibilities. Only after these responsibilities are appropriately assumed do privileges follow. J. Dunn found that positive interaction by the parents with each child is one of the major factors in minimizing sibling rivalry. She found that the mother was particularly important in this role.[4] When each child is treated equally, fairly, and in an age-appropriate manner by their parents, siblings will interact optimally. Clear family rules and expectations for each child also enhance this behavior. Teaching children about taking turns, delineation of property, and who will do which chores, also reduces their frustrations. Clear instruction regarding specific responsibilities can minimize bickering and fighting over these issues.

These four variables mentioned above: birth order, the quality of the parenting relationship, competition for property, and the quality of overall family interaction, as well as the individual personalities of each child, explain the great complexity of sibling relationships. A better understanding of these will help us to develop the most appropriate strategy for our children.

TREATMENT STRATEGIES

There are a number of parenting approaches from which to choose in dealing with sibling rivalry. The laissez-faire approach to sibling rivalry involves sitting back, doing nothing, and letting the children fend for themselves. Besides being unfair, this approach has disastrous effects on the family. King David in the Bible painfully realized this. David was successful with almost everything he attempted in life. He was a great warrior, poet, musician, and king, but he was a failure as a father. The main reason seemed to be that he did not spend time with his children. He left that job for others. The disastrous results included a son who raped his half sister, the murder of that son by another son, who later tried to dethrone his father, and extreme competition between sons over who would be the next king prior to David's death. If David were alive today, he would probably discourage parents from using a laissez-faire approach with their children.

A firm and decisive approach to sibling rivalry can be vital. When there is conflict between younger siblings, planned interventions can often separate the children quickly. These interventions have to be implemented repeatedly because children of this age have limited reasoning ability and they forget quickly. Effective consequences for a preschool child include isolation in one's room, standing in the corner, or assignments of work around the house or yard.

Suppose older brother is playing with some building blocks, and younger sister comes along. All of a sudden, there is a loud "boom." Everything starts to deteriorate, including the interaction between the two siblings. How can parents handle this situation? First, an expression of your sympathy to the older child can aid in reducing the desire to retaliate. Restraining the younger sibling verbally or physically often keeps him or her from further destroying any of older brother's world. Wait until the children are calm enough to listen, and talk about what each child feels and needs, if appropriate. If the younger child is a toddler, explain his or her limitations to the oldest child. Explain that younger siblings often do not understand, they are curious, they like to explore, they knock things down, and they sometimes just cannot help what they do. Next, provide a high table top or separate space where the older child can play in peace. Tell older brother that at times he can play on the floor if he does not mind his blocks being knocked over. This calm, matter-of-fact approach to handling sibling rivalry can be extremely important.

As siblings become older, the direct approach becomes more difficult. Parents must learn to become mediators who will help children resolve conflicts for themselves. For instance, suppose two school-age children are arguing about who is going to play in the driveway. The first statement could be something like this, "It seems as if the two of you have a problem. What do you think we can do about it?"

If the children start screaming and yelling accusations, simply inform them that there will be no playing in the driveway for either of them until they calm down and find a solution. (Stick to your word!) After much negotiating and different ideas from the children, they may come up with the idea of letting each person play on the driveway by themselves for an allotted period of time or sharing the area together. With older children, the likelihood of peace is often greater when the children have come up with a solution themselves.

Treat each child as unique, special, important, and as an individual. Although there are times for the whole family to interact and be together, find times when you can interact with children according to their own interests. One child may like playing basketball, another would rather go shopping, while another child would simply like to go eat at a restaurant. Try to find that special, individual time. During these times, be complimentary toward him, and let him know his strong points—ways you appreciate him, and ways you would like to see him develop. In this way, the parent can further meet each child's needs outside the whole family group. It is important to make sure that each child has special time with each parent.

LESSON FROM GENESIS 4

Genesis 4 provides numerous lessons about sibling rivalry. It is important for parents to look at the modeling of God and the way he handled this sibling rivalry.

First of all, God inquired about Cain's emotions: "Why are you angry?" Parents also need to help the children express their emotions in a way that would not be hurtful to other people. Let the children know that you want to know how they feel.

God also used reasoning with Cain: "If you do what is right." It is important to use reasoning with our children. Explain to them the reasons why certain standards of interaction exist within the family. Help them to develop their own individual reasoning process. Explain to them the reasons why it is important for brothers and sisters to get along with each other.

God was active in teaching Cain: "You must master it." Our family uses family devotions as a teaching time every morning before the children leave for school. In our devotionals we discuss numerous topics. Sibling rivalry and some of the underlying aspects of sibling rivalry can be dealt with in this kind of teaching atmosphere. Parents should use practical examples from the Scriptures and daily life in the family devotions. One example is Jesus' response to the sibling rivalry of his disciples (Matt. 20:20-27). Jesus encouraged them to be servants.

Several years ago, our family completed a three-week series of family devotionals on the topic of being servants. We noticed a great change in behavior as a result of going through the Bible and looking up examples of people who served. Some great family discussions can be built around the following passages of Scripture: Matthew 18:15-20; Matthew 18:21-35; Matthew 5:24; Matthew 7:4; Luke 12:13-21; and Proverbs 17:17.

God disciplined the wrongdoer. In this case, God definitely punished Cain. When one sibling is definitely in the wrong, then parents need to make sure that this behavior is disciplined.

WHEN EXASPERATED

In spite of all the great mediating techniques, there will be times when children will not even cooperate with this system and will need to be disciplined. There are times when your children will not resolve an issue, and their anger only escalates. In this situation, you may discipline both siblings by sending them to different parts of the house or yard to think and meditate for twenty or thirty minutes. In other cases, it may be just one sibling who is responsible. This sibling should be disciplined in a manner that matches the offense. Children should never be allowed to hit, fight, or harm each other. In our family, this aggressive, hurtful behavior is disciplined quickly and automatically.

COOPERATION

Make cooperation a family password. Build the feeling that, "We are a family and help one another." Maybe this is why Big Bird on Sesame Street is so popular with young children. He stands for cooperation. Parents can set the example in cooperation. We can help our children with tasks and help them do tasks cooperatively. Our family has Saturday chores, and each family member must participate. I often put a sign on the TV that says, "No TV until chores are completed." This allows children to feel a part of the family by knowing that their task is important and must be completed before free time.

STRATEGY MEETING

Have a strategy meeting. My wife and I go out to eat every Saturday, and two topics we often discuss are how to deal with sibling rivalry and the children's individual needs. This kind of communication can produce great results in family cooperation. It gives us, as parents, an opportunity to define needs and decide what, or who, requires attention most. Our "ace in the hole" for dealing with intense rivalry is the special relaxing time my wife and I have alone. Time taken to rest and relax can refresh and invigorate couples for the task of mediating sibling rivalry disputes.

"TIME OUT"

Set the kitchen timer or use a stop watch for calming time when siblings act up and must sit apart from each other. This saves the parent from becoming part of the argument. If arguing or bickering continues, then a stronger measure is needed next time.

PRAYER

Pray for wisdom to know how to handle sibling rivalry. God is the ultimate source of wisdom, and he can give us the wisdom to know what to do in each situation.

ROLE-PLAY

Learn to role-play sibling interactions. Our family role-played different situations on a recent vacation trip. It not only helped each child to see how the other person felt, but it was a hilariously fun time.

LISTEN

Closely listen to disputes. Ask questions, restate the problem, cultivate a mutual understanding, pray, give full courtesy and respect to each child. Do not just assume what the feelings are of each individual child. Avoid interrupting, try to answer all questions, and determine what each child really needs. The following are some excellent Proverbs to study: Proverbs 18:13; 28:21, 25; 30:32-33; 26:17-19; 24:23-25. Parents' obedience of these proverbs will produce excellent results.

INTERVIEW

Interview each child about specific situations and ask each of them questions about how they feel. My seven-year-old son's response to what caused problems between brothers and sisters was simply, "arguments." My ten-year-old daughter stated that she thought the cause of sibling rivalry stemmed from "one person trying to look out for the other person's business too much." She says, "One person sees only the wrong in the other person and not the good." Her advice was, "Don't stick your nose in each other's business and don't boss each other." She also felt strongly that brothers and sisters should not deliberately tease each other. Her advice to parents was to listen to both sides and then decide what was best. Interviewing our children can help us create better strategies for dealing with sibling rivalry.

CONTRACTS

Siblings can make a mutual agreement. When there is a problem, the atmosphere needs to be positive. Help the children define their goals and allow plenty of time for discussion.

Make a contract between siblings, and then have it documented in writing. Each child should state what he/she wants to do differently and the goals he/she wants to achieve. Each child can sign the contract, and then it can be posted where all can review it as needed. Schedule a time when the contract can be reevaluated on a periodic basis.

UNDERSTANDING BIRTH ORDER

Understanding how the firstborn, the middle child, and the youngest child normally react in families is a great help in planning strategies to meet their needs. The oldest child is typically perfectionistic, reliable, conscientious, a list maker, well organized, critical, serious, and scholarly. The middle child is usually a mediator, has the fewest pictures in the family photo album, avoids conflict, is independent, is extremely loyal to the peer group, has many friends, and is often a maverick. The youngest child can be manipulative, charming, precocious, engaging, a clown, and very people-oriented. In order to get detailed information on how to help your children, see *The Birth Order Book* by Dr. Kevin Leman.

CONCLUSION

Sibling rivalry is rough! However, it can be controlled and minimized by good husband-wife communication and clear ideas on how to help the children work out their differences. Each strategy should be carefully studied and prayed about. Prayer, communication, and putting into practice these strategies are important in order to have joyful family relationships. Then, someday, your children can say, "Sibs are not sub, but super!"

3
Fathers and Sons
D. Charles Williams

It is not easy for a boy to become a man today. It takes men to build men, and too often they are just not available. It appears that fathers have become a scarce commodity in this busy decade. The challenge of most men in their thirties and forties is to make their professional mark and establish themselves financially. Ironically, this is precisely the time when our young children need us the most.

One successful middle-aged businessman once commented to another, "I'd give any amount of money to have a family like yours."

To this the successful father replied, "That's exactly what it takes . . . giving up any amount of money!"

If most fathers were asked, "Which is more important to you, your family or your job?" they would quickly affirm the importance of the family. Yet it would be evident to an outside objective observer that most men's time, energy, and interests are directed toward other areas. The psalm writer said, "Sons are a heritage from the Lord, children a reward from him. Like arrows in the hands of a warrior are sons born in one's youth. Blessed is the man whose quiver is full of them" (Ps. 127:3-5).

Being too busy is one of the most unfortunate mistakes a father can make with his children. One insightful wife said to her hurried husband who was being pestered by his children for attention, "Don't worry, in a few years they won't be around to bother you."

Fathers have such a tremendous opportunity and responsibility to shape the attitudes and lives of their children, especially their sons. My mother showed me unconditional love, acceptance, and forgiveness, but my father taught me determination, character, and most of all, how to be a man. Perhaps the most significant relationship in a young boy's life is the influence his father has upon shaping his identity as a male. I grew up in a family with three sons, and now I am the father of two sons. The influence my life potentially has upon these boys is a responsibility that seems overwhelming at times. Fathers who do not realize how their relationship with their sons affects their future often look back with regret at their shortsightedness. The most successful coach in college football, the University of Alabama's Bear Bryant, said shortly before his death, "I wish I had been a better Christian and family man."

THE REEMERGING FATHER

The importance of the father-son relationship has received almost no attention in the literature of the last decade or more. However, fatherhood in general has reemerged out of necessity with the growing prevalence of two-career and single-parent families.

Fathers continually walk a fine line between under-responsibility and overresponsibility. If a father concentrates too much on being a buddy to his son, some may call him weak or indulgent. If he becomes a strict disciplinarian, he runs the risk of being viewed by his son as an ogre. If he has done well financially and gives his children the material benefits he lacked, he is spoiling them and failing to prepare them for the real world. If he is wealthy but does not give to them materially the way other fathers do, he gains the reputation for being stingy. If his job keeps him away often, he is shirking his fatherly responsibilities and may find that his wife resents him and his children no longer seem to need him.

The fine line between being the guide and mentor to one's son and sharing that responsibility with one's wife is a difficult job for any well-intentioned father. American males, for the most part, are unprepared when it comes to learning and being encouraged about their fatherly roles. Little girls are taught to become "mommies" from an early age, while sons are encouraged to protect, defend, and provide in materialistic ways. It is no wonder their priorities are so easily confused. Needless to say, this in no way reduces our responsibility as men to understand the deep emotional needs of our sons so that this problem is not carried on to the next generation. Therefore, it is very important for the father-son relationship to receive the attention it so desperately deserves so that this upcoming generation of men can learn from our example how to appropriately father their sons.

The god of this decade is success. The "success motive" is responsible for countless fathers selling out to provide more materially for their families. The allurement to gain reputation and social standing is often insidious in its effect, if not overwhelming. The result of losing sight of one's priorities is felt minimally at first, but often tragically years later. Ironically, the financial security, status, and position attained come at the cost of the family's well-being. While the father's intentions as a provider are good, he is inadvertently teaching his son by his example to repeat the same mistakes.

On a regular basis, middle-aged successful families come into my office trying to recapture missed opportunities for emotional closeness and unity. While they are financially secure, many generally feel emotionally deprived. Ironically, the goal of financial security has been accomplished at the cost of emotional security and often results in divorce, troubled youths, family embarrassment, and disappointment.

There is no shortcut to becoming a success as a husband, father, and provider. Fathers who think differently do so at the expense of their marriages and relationships with their children. Sons need fathers to show them that real success comes from loving Jesus Christ first, the family second, and the job third.

Fathers who have ignored their sons for years often discover them to be very angry and rebellious as teenagers. Paul in Colossians implored fathers not to embitter their children, or they could become discouraged (3:21). Some try to identify with their fathers at a very early age. If fathers ignore those needs, sons often interpret this as rejection. While this may be inadvertent or unintentional, the end result is still the same—a feeling of isolation and abandonment.

When a father is too busy, minimally affectionate, quiet, or allows others or activities to take priority over time with his sons, a silent message becomes loud and clear: *"You are not as important, worthwhile, or valuable as these other interests."* In response to this, some sons rebel and become just the opposite of what their fathers would approve. Others try diligently throughout their life to be a "Xerox copy" of what they think their father would want, yet to no avail. Still others drift from relationship to relationship seeking the close, emotional validation and approval from other men or father figures throughout their lives. This is one of the allurements that occasionally draws young men into homosexual relationships.

It has probably been underestimated until now the strong significance of fathers taking the time their sons need to identify with them as males, as leaders, as fathers, and as nurturing human beings. As the role of the father reemerges with its significance upon the family, the father-son relationship must be examined for its influence upon the son's identity. This relationship has far-reaching implications for the future development of family life.

LEARNING FROM EXPERIENCE— FATHERS AND SONS IN HISTORY

"Wear shoes you want filled" is the title to a chapter of a book, *The Effective Father,* which discusses the importance of a father's example. It is absolutely true that sons do follow in the steps of their fathers, beginning at an early age. Several years ago, I walked into the kitchen only to discover both my sons standing there in a pair of my over-sized shoes. When they saw me they both laughed excitedly as if to say, "Look, Dad, we're just like you." My wife ran to get the camera to take a picture of this very funny occasion.

In retrospect, the significance of that scene sobers me. My sons are beginning to imitate and "fill my shoes" even now. When children are young, parents tend to tell them how to live the best life. Yet children often close their ears and minds to what is said and watch closely what is done. Sons will generally do what a father says until they become teenagers, and then do what their fathers do. Occasionally, we hear people jokingly say, "Do as I say, not as I do," and we immediately realize the futility of this statement. If a father wants to better understand his son, he should ask himself this question: "What is there about me that my son is copying?" John wrote to his friend Gaius, "I have no greater joy than to hear that my children are walking in the truth" (3 John 4). This can only be true in the life of a son if he is following his father's footsteps as his father is following Jesus Christ.

One morning at breakfast when my oldest son was three years old, I finished my meal, picked up my plate, put it in the sink, kissed my wife, said, "Thanks, Babe," and walked out of the room. Several seconds later, Christopher got down from his chair, picked up his plate, reached up and put it on the counter, kissed his mother, waved his hand, and said, "Thanks, Babe," as he walked to the den to watch cartoons. What a valuable lesson I learned from observing this brief scene!

If a father does not want his son to repeat certain mistakes he has made, it is essential for that father to change his own behavior, his attitude, and at times, his character as it relates to that shortcoming. There are many examples in the Bible of sons who were very much like their fathers, for better or worse. Abram and his wife, Sarai, traveled to Egypt to live there for a while because of the famine (Gen. 12). Abram's wife was so beautiful, he feared the Egyptians might kill him and take her. He therefore lied and said that she was his sister so they would be treated well. Abram's fears were unfounded, but his dishonesty caused the pharaoh and his household a great deal of trouble. Later in life, Abraham had a son named Isaac. In Genesis 26, another famine occurred, and Isaac was instructed to go to Egypt temporarily with his wife, Rebekah. Ironically, Isaac had the same fear his father had. Because of Rebekah's beauty, he lied and identified her as his sister so they would not be killed. Isn't it amazing that Abraham's fears and manner of handling this particular problem were somehow passed on and repeated by his son Isaac?

The best example of a father-son relationship, of course, is that of Jesus Christ and God the Father. Throughout the Scriptures, we observe Jesus praying to his Father every day. He got up early, stayed up late, and spoke with him at various times throughout his day. Jesus respected and obeyed his Father because he knew how much his Father loved him. God's eye was always upon Jesus. He had confidence in Jesus to handle the responsibilities he was given. God was well pleased with his Son and told him so (Luke 3:22). He also told others to listen to Jesus. Jesus imitated his Father and made the Father's will his will. He felt "one" with his Father. They were so close that they were the same. God was always ready to provide whatever Jesus needed—support, the right words to say, insight into difficult situations, the power to persevere, and the love that overcomes fear.

Paul and Timothy had a spiritual father-son relationship, too. Paul wrote, "To Timothy, my true son in the faith" (1 Tim. 1:2). Timothy was viewed earlier in his spiritual life as timid, shy, and physically frail. Paul, on the other hand, was known for his strength, determination, and drive to know Christ. Paul was able to influence Timothy in a fatherly way because of his love and devotion. Because of Timothy's mild and fearful disposition, one would expect that he would have had a difficult time being involved and concerned with others. Yet, Paul talked about how he had no one else like Timothy who took a genuine interest in the welfare of others (Phil. 2:20). Due to Paul's influence, Timothy had proven himself and had allowed God's power to change his basic nature. All sons need fathers who can turn their weaknesses into strengths.

Eli had been appointed by God to be a priest at the tabernacle at Shiloh, a very responsible position that took a great deal of time and energy. During his lifetime, Eli had allowed his sons to help him with his priestly responsibilities. After a time, he apparently lost touch with them and was unaware of the direction in which their characters had developed. It was not until Eli was very old that he heard from other sources that his sons were helping themselves to the sacrifices and were sleeping with the women who served at the entrance to the Tent of Meeting.

It was a shame that Eli was not more involved with his sons and that he did not sense their unholy attitudes. Eli approached his sons and asked them, "Why do you do such things?" (1 Sam. 2:23). Unfortunately, Eli was ineffectively questioning their behavior instead of influencing it. Eli apparently did not assert his responsibility as a priest and a father, for his sons did not listen to him. Finally, God asked Eli, "Why do you honor your sons more than me by fattening yourselves on the choice parts of every offering made by my people Israel?" Even after God's inquiry, Eli was unsuccessful in intervening and changing his sons' behavior. The final outcome for his inattention was the death of his sons and himself.

Eli's problem as a father was that he was uninvolved with his sons regularly. He did not monitor their behavior, and he failed to take action to correct their mistakes. Eli did not deal with their attitudes and their hearts. Neither did he persist until they listened to him. Because of Eli's leniency, God held him responsible and retracted the promise of priesthood from his family line. God considered Eli's lack of supervision over his sons as actually choosing them over him. Eli unintentionally became a party to the death of his sons and himself by his lack of involvement in their lives. How many fathers are so busy they are unaware of their sons' attitudes and behavior! It is so disconcerting to hear from friends or to read in the paper about children of respectable people in the community getting into trouble! We often think to ourselves how pitiful this is and then later in life find ourselves in the same predicament.

David was a "man after God's own heart." During his younger years, he served God with a great deal of devotion. Unfortunately, he became so responsible and busy that he could not effectively attend to the needs of his family. During the most responsible period of David's career, his spiritual commitment to God was weakened. Later, David became involved with Bathsheba (2 Sam. 11). From this time on, David had continual problems with his family. David's son Amnon raped his half sister Tamar. In response to this, her brother Absalom had Amnon killed. Later, Absalom tried to take his father's throne from him and was killed in the process. When David was older, his son Adonijah also tried to take his throne from him. The writer of 1 Kings stated that his father had never interfered with him by asking, "Why do you behave as you do?" (1:6). Because Solomon was in line for the throne, he had

Adonijah put to death. Solomon himself later drifted from God and took many wives. And so, it seems that David was a success in his career but a failure as a father.

The successes and failures of these fathers are examples from which we can all learn. In most cases, the problem was not what a son was taught, but whether his father was regularly involved with him and made certain he followed through with the appropriate motivation and attitude. The most successful fathers teach the truth, set the example, and monitor their children's behavior. Anything less than this is ineffective fathering.

WHAT FATHERS TEACH THEIR SONS

There are at least four areas in which a father can teach his son how to become a man. These areas include loving God and becoming Christ-like, cultivating manliness, being a responsible leader and initiator, sharing feelings, and communicating needs. Each of these areas is essential if a son is to develop his potential to the fullest.

Loving God and Becoming More Christ-like. If our sons are to grow up loving God and putting their faith in him, they must see us as fathers doing the same thing. When more time, energy, and enthusiasm is directed in other areas, it does not take long for a young son to realize what is most important in his father's life. It has been said that a young child at two is your master, at ten is your slave, at fifteen is your double, and after that, your friend or foe depending on how you brought him up. If we bring our sons up loving God and imitating Christ, they will follow that example.

When our sons were very young, my wife read them Bible stories out of children's books. We began the practice of reading these stories each morning at the breakfast table. As they have grown older, I have begun using specific parables, stories, and examples out of the Bible. The selec-

tion of the Bible study each morning is based on my sons'
behavior the day before or their attitudes that morning.
For instance, if they have difficulty listening to us, we might
study Numbers 22, Balaam and the donkey. In this story,
Balaam refuses to listen to God until his donkey speaks to
him and helps him see how disobedient he has been.
Likewise, if we are concentrating on the boys' behavior
that day, we might study Matthew 12:33 about "good fruit
and bad fruit." Matthew 12:43 is a good example of temporarily changing behavior and not changing one's heart.
In this passage, an evil spirit leaves a house and the house
is put back in order, yet permanent changes are not made,
and the final condition of the house is worse than the first.
When discussing how our sons talk to each other or to
their friends, we might use Ephesians 4:29, which discour-
ages unwholesome talk and encourages "only what is helpful for building others up according to their needs."

By beginning each day with a story relevant to their own
needs and behavior, they can go through each day focused
upon specific issues they practically apply in their own
lives. It is so vitally important that fathers take the lead in
relating these stories and in asking them questions to make
sure they understand the meaning and application to their
own lives.

It is also important to teach our sons the importance of
personal Bible study and prayer. This can easily be done
by allowing them to observe us having a daily Bible study
and prayer time. One morning when my oldest son was
two years old, I discovered him kneeling beside my bed
as I was praying with his hands folded as if he was praying
also. On another occasion, I found him sitting in his room
with his children's Bible opened looking at the pictures.
He was having his own Bible study "just like Daddy."

A particularly fun time for fathers and sons can be preparing for bed. Each evening, we end the day by taking turns
praying. We talk about upcoming events. This allows for
personal time together, demonstrations of affection, and
little talks about matters on our minds. Moses wrote,

> *Hear, O Israel: The Lord our God, the Lord is one.*
> *Love the Lord your God with all your heart and with*
> *all your soul and with all your strength. These com-*
> *mandments that I give you today are to be upon*
> *your hearts. Impress them on your children. Talk*
> *about them when you sit at home and when you*
> *walk along the road, when you lie down and when*
> *you get up. Tie them as symbols on your hands and*
> *bind them on your foreheads. Write them on the door-*
> *frames of your house and on your gates. (Deut. 6:4-9)*

Fathers who make the time to be with their sons every day truly show them how to love God and how to imitate Jesus Christ.

Cultivating Manliness. Fathers teach boys how to be men. This takes time, energy, and personal involvement. It is so disheartening to see sons take on too many of the gestures and characteristics of their mothers simply because fathers have not been around. Fathers teach their sons to like themselves and to feel worthwhile. The father who is constantly correcting and criticizing his son is inadvertently undermining his own self-confidence. Self-esteem is slowly built by accentuating strengths and praising any sign of effort and progress noted.

It is vital for a father to take the time to help his son develop coordination through physical and athletic games. Even if a father is not athletic himself, early exposure to these games builds agility and confidence. It also teaches our sons camaraderie and how to participate as part of a team. This sense of belonging helps our sons make friends more easily and develop loyalty.

My own father is perhaps the best example of a man who took specific time out to teach my brothers and me how to throw, catch, and bat a baseball, and how to catch and kick a football. More importantly, he taught us that practice makes perfect, not to overreact to injuries, and never to give up.

Fathers also need to have male friends themselves in order to teach their sons the importance of friendship. Many men today do not have best friends, but only casual acquaintances. This pattern in fathers is an example that sons will very readily follow.

Fathers should also teach their sons how to handle their tempers. Self-control is one of the most difficult qualities to master. If a father has never learned to be patient himself, he will see his son grow to be an impatient young man. Our world is full of men who are still little boys in some respects because they have been unable to master certain weaknesses and impulses in their lives.

It is also important that children be able to defend themselves when in danger of physical harm as did David with Goliath and later with Saul. We should follow Christ's example by "turning the other cheek" and by avoiding the aggressions of others as he did when the crowd tried to throw him off the cliff in Luke 4:28. The purpose of self-defense is not to infringe upon someone else's rights, but to have the confidence and assurance to protect oneself and one's family if necessary.

My oldest son takes karate in order to learn discipline, confidence, and self-control, and I hope my younger son will get involved also. The son who has been taught the proper balance of emotions, to discipline his body, and to have confidence in himself has truly begun to cultivate manliness.

Developing Responsible Leadership Abilities. In life, it is necessary for a man to learn responsibility and discipline. If he is unable to organize himself, attempts to maintain a family will often be frustrating. The writer of Proverbs said, "Discipline your son in his early years when there is hope; if you don't you will ruin his life" (19:18). Families with fathers who are ineffective leaders face constant trouble similar to a leaderless athletic team that often loses. As children become developmentally able to perform certain tasks around the home, they should be taught to dress themselves, keep their room clean, and handle various chores that are their responsibility.

Children should also be taught the importance of handling money. Some parents disagree with the plan of giving allowances, feeling that if a child is regularly completing his chores, money should be provided if the child's need for money is legitimate. Our family prefers to allot a weekly allowance. Part of it the children give to God as a contribution, another part is saved, and the remaining amount can be spent as they choose. If sons learn good money management habits at an early age, they will be less likely to learn by mistakes later in life. Fathers who allow their sons to spend all of their money on anything they choose are condoning habits that may be difficult to change in later years. Men are called upon to provide for their families, and helping them manage an allowance can teach them from the beginning that everything they earn is not theirs to do with as they choose.

Young boys and men in our society are often placed in the position of being initiators. Males must become comfortable meeting people, asking for jobs, asking for dates, and taking a number of risks throughout their lives. Fathers can best teach their sons to do this by their attitude of determination and perseverance. Fathers who are fearful or who are reluctant to try new things will inadvertently teach their sons to be mere spectators in the game of life. If fathers have a subtle fear of failure that is not challenged and overcome, it may also become difficult for the sons to effectively manage life's pressures. Patience and optimism are invaluable traits for a child to model from his father.

Paul cited the three most important attitudes to have in life: "faith, hope, and love" (1 Cor. 13). When a father truly believes and practices Romans 8:28, his son will also grow up to believe that, "All things work to the good of those who love the Lord and are called according to his purpose." Many opportunities are available in life for the person who is willing to initiate. As with anything new in life, there are risks to be taken, but the experience gained and the confidence acquired by merely trying something different is worth it.

Communicating Needs and Feelings. Of all the areas previously discussed, this is perhaps the most difficult for men. We often mistakenly ascribe feelings, communication, and needs to the woman's role. Somehow these qualities don't seem "macho" enough, and men try to stay away from them like a bad cold. Yet, a man who does not understand his own feelings or emotional needs and, worse yet, is unable to communicate them is quite an isolated person. As men, we have often been encouraged to deny these needs, and yet we wonder why we are accused of being insensitive toward others.

By realizing that real masculinity is a balance of strength and gentleness, perhaps we can exorcise the demonic myth that "tenderness is a weakness." Of course, some men go too far to the other extreme of being too sensitive, maintaining no opinions about anything, and constantly deferring to the preferences of their wives. In my view, this is true weakness. The father who teaches the importance of communicating his true emotional needs will develop a son who is sensitive to his future wife and children.

HOMOSEXUALITY

Homosexuality is a problem that has confused and repulsed people for many years. Young men who feel these urges and attractions to other men are often very confused, while other men who have never experienced these feelings are generally threatened and repulsed by the very thought of them. It is not within the scope of this chapter to fully explore the causes and problems of homosexuality, but several key issues need to be examined.

To begin, homosexuality is primarily an identity problem.

This means that a young boy begins at an early age having difficulties appropriately identifying with his father, or a young girl has difficulties with her mother. It often begins so early that many homosexuals will maintain that they never had a choice and were destined to that life-style. This simply is not the case. While many past researchers have noted the classic parental pattern for men of a dominant, engulfing mother and a weak, distant father, there are several other potential family combinations that can contribute to homosexuality.

One factor that is often overlooked in males is the father-son relationship. In almost every case where I have counseled a gay male, the father-son relationship has experienced problems. With many of these clients, they are not looking for a sexual relationship but for closeness, security, strength, and protection. Many of them have even eventually stated that they have been, in effect, "looking for Daddy." It is no wonder in their search for emotional validation and security that sexual involvement becomes a confusing factor.

Fathers who reject their sons because of their homosexuality have failed to see through the problem to the real heart of the issue. They need to be loved by a strong, caring, accepting father. Homosexual males that reject their fathers because of past misunderstandings cause themselves to miss out on one of the possible solutions to their confused identity problem. By finally feeling accepted by their dads and accepting their fathers in return, the beginning of the journey toward feeling secure as a man can begin.

RECOMMENDATIONS FOR FATHERS AND SONS

With the amount of media coverage and reading material available to fathers today, it is unnecessary for us as fathers to make all the mistakes our fathers made in rearing us. Yet, it is difficult to determine what philosophy is the best to follow. The father who loves Jesus with all his heart, who realizes that this is his first attempt at childrearing, who accepts that he is a fallible human being, and who uses a generous amount of love and patience has a high probability of succeeding as an effective father. Fathers and sons need to talk regularly, clearly, and directly. If a father is easily able to admit and apologize for his mistakes in judgment, sons can understand more readily how difficult a job being a father is. Listening can never be underrated.

Most of us talk twice as much as we listen even though we are anatomically equipped to do just the opposite. Being "listened to" and "feeling heard" creates the understanding that most of us need to emotionally open up and learn from our mistakes.

Fathers need to allow their sons to grow up, and sons need to allow their fathers to grow up. Fathers err by continuing to see their adult sons as little boys. How difficult it is for us to let go of our earlier images of when our son or father was younger! A new relationship begins when fathers and sons are able to forgive the past and view each other more in the present in an accepting manner. This gives the relationship an opportunity to correct itself and grow into a real friendship.

Fathers and sons can find it very profitable to talk about the past and how they view the future of their relationship. If a father and son can relate to each other in the present as equals, the relationship can evolve in later life to a mutually mature love and appreciation for one another. Yet, fathers and sons need not wait until later life to enjoy this kind of relationship. Foresight, attention, affection, discipline, and example can give any father and son a head start on making that relationship all it was meant to be.

4

Verbally Oppositional Behavior in Children
D. Charles Williams, Ph.D.

INTRODUCTION

As parents, ideally we hope our children are appreciative, polite, tactful, honest, kind, and patient in all they say and do. This, however, is not the state in which our "little bundles of joy" arrive into the world. Our job as parents, then, is to instill in them these qualities gradually through diligent teaching and example during their developmental years.

Verbally oppositional behavior is one of the most important but often ignored areas of a child's upbringing. For instance, a five- or six-year-old child who whines to get his mother's attention, argues until he has his way, complains when he has to settle for something less than he requested, interrupts most conversations Mom and Dad try to have, and talks back to his parents, is unpleasant to be around. He is also often unhappy with himself and well on his way to becoming a dissatisfied pessimist who is difficult to please, no matter how hard someone else tries. As parents, "our mission, should we choose to accept it," is to be confident and clear enough as to what we want from our children to convince them of those expectations.

As adults, we often find ourselves responding with a "squeaky wheel mentality" or to the "tyranny of the urgent." During our day-to-day routine at the office, in social affairs, or at home, whoever or whatever makes the most commotion gets our immediate attention, even though it may have lesser importance than some other priority. Children do not need a degree in child development or parent psychology to realize when a parent will spring into action over their demands. When we as parents find ourselves responding in this fashion, we are unwittingly and usually unconsciously training our children to be our masters. On the other hand, it is also quite true that children who are shipped off each day to school, to day care, or to another child-care facility, and who come home at the end of the day only to be ignored will often use these tactics to acquire negative attention. For them, negative attention is better than none at all.

In my office recently, a family called requesting an emergency appointment because their eight-year-old son had run away from home. As they sat in the session discussing why young Jimmy had left on this ten-mile journey to his aunt's house to "live forever," the real issues began to emerge. Jimmy's plans to accompany his father to softball practice had been canceled because the older men were going to eat dinner afterwards. On the next day when Jimmy asked his father to "play catch" in the backyard, his father was too tired. His allowance had also been taken away from him for acting up when he did not want to be left with a babysitter earlier that week. Jimmy, like most kids, did not want to be ignored, and rather than be overlooked, ran away so that his parents would have to find him and finally listen to what he was saying.

Verbally oppositional behavior is not limited to any one age group. For instance, all mothers become acutely aware of the meaning behind the types of different cries their infants make. They know when their child is hungry, wet, hurt, or angry by the tone and the intensity of the baby's crying. Toddlers can also cause their parents to spring into action when they want something to eat, insist upon a harmful object they should not have, or whine until they are picked up. Teenagers also at times engage their parents in oppositional repartee, argue that their parent's treatment of them is unfair, resort to the silent treatment, or occasionally regress into name-calling. Adults who are inclined more toward running commentaries on what's wrong with *this* person or *that* situation may also risk becoming negative, pessimistic, or even chronic complainers.

Clearly, then, it is never too early or too late to address this problem of verbally oppositional behavior. The results of ignoring it, however, can be devastating to our family and all those around us for a lifetime.

ARGUING, WHINING, AND COMPLAINING

This type of verbally oppositional behavior becomes a problem in our families for a number of reasons. From the beginning, parents feel a great deal of responsibility for the care and nurturing of their children. Similarly, children are extremely dependent upon their parents to have their personal needs met. Of course, our objective as parents is to help our children become less, not more, dependent upon us. However, it does not take long for children to realize that there is a great deal of power in weakness. When children cannot do something effectively, their cries of frustration quickly activate their parents to help them solve their dilemma. Children soon realize that their weaknesses can be easily remedied by demanding our intervention as parents. This, however, does not teach them to cope with the frustrations of learning things for themselves, and moreover keeps them tied to us in an unhealthy, dependent way.

Parents who give in too easily to their children's demands can unintentionally disable their children's motivation to learn and stifle their developing self-confidence. Children who have a lot done for them, or given to them, often become unappreciative and thankless, expecting their parents to meet their every request. These same children are also frequently seen treating their parents in a disrespectful manner.

Parents sometimes contribute to such arguing, complaining, or whining when they themselves model this behavior. An adult who is easily irritated or who gets impatient with his spouse, traffic, or interruptions, teaches by example. Parents who tolerate this kind of behavior in themselves are condoning a habit that will be extremely difficult for them to change in their children when they grow older.

It is true that children go through different developmental stages during which their tolerance for frustration is lower. These times, however, are also opportunities to learn from mistakes. Parents' mature handling of their own frustrations can help their children accept difficulties as a legitimate part of life while modeling specific ways to resolve them.

Parents who are too busy, and dismiss this behavior as a passing stage, may find that it continues and worsens indefinitely. Arguing and complaining may be a request for attention from the parent in a way that the child knows cannot be ignored. When our children are well-behaved and preoccupied quietly in other activities, though, it is often easy to forget that they need regular and consistent time and attention from us. When they are frequently ignored by us, they question their value in our eyes, and feelings of inferiority may arise. Their constant expressions of dissatisfaction for other things may be symptomatic of their feelings of inferiority about themselves. Children who have little interaction with their parents easily lose their zest for life and often act apathetic and pessimistic. Our regular involvement and genuine interest in their feelings and activities reassures them of their worth to us.

Finally, arguing and complaining may be an attempt to avoid responsibility or an effort to get out of something they have been requested to do. If we suspect this to be the case, reiterate the request, again stating the importance of each family member doing his share. Should opposition continue, ask the child if he would prefer more work in addition to the original job. If cooperation has not been accomplished at this point, begin including additional responsibilities with each rebuttal. Of course, fairness and the free expression of feelings should be encouraged, but when this is used as a platform to debate and manipulate, the above tactics are very effective.

Before these types of verbally oppositional behavior in children can be effectively remedied, their cause must be identified. Are they tired, frustrated, lonely, insecure, too dependent, or feeling unhappy with themselves? It is usually important to make an assessment of the motives behind their behavior before an effective intervention technique can be implemented.

INTERVENTIONS FOR MANAGING ARGUING, WHINING, AND COMPLAINING

Stop It! It is important for children to have the freedom within a family to voice their opinions, express their feelings, and air their differences. This allows them to feel a part of the process of decision making and to understand the final outcome. However, parents ultimately have the last word. When a child continues to disagree, chatter incessantly, and behave oppositionally, the privilege of dialogue among family members has been abused. Paul instructed, "Turn away from godless chatter and the opposing ideas of what is falsely called knowledge, which some have professed and in so doing have wandered from the faith" (1 Tim. 6:20).

The first responsibility of a parent who is confronted with this type of conflict is to tactfully "stop it." It is important for parents to guide their children on to maturity so that they can pursue what it right and live in peace with other people. The apostle Paul warned:

> *Flee the evil desires of youth, and pursue righteous-
> ness, faith, love and peace, along with all those who
> call on the Lord out of a pure heart. Don't have
> anything to do with foolish and stupid arguments,
> because you know they produce quarrels. And the
> Lord's servant must not quarrel; instead, he must be
> kind to everyone, able to teach, not resentful. Those
> who oppose him he must gently instruct, in the hope
> that God will grant them repentance leading them
> to a knowledge of the truth, and that they will come
> to their senses and escape from the trap of the devil,
> who has taken them captive to do his will. (2 Tim.
> 2:22)*

The child who learns to trust his parent's judgment will
develop a pure heart. Quarreling generally leads to unkind
behavior and eventually resentment. The parent who gently
instructs his child, not allowing him to argue unnecessarily,
will lead him to the knowledge of the truth. Children often
require more time to understand the reasoning behind
decisions, yet with patience and persistence, they can come
to their senses and escape the all-too-human tendency to
become cantankerous and complainers.

Teach Cause and Effect. We adults often miss opportunities
to learn from our mistakes because we have not taken the
time to analyze what has contributed to the moods and
emotions we have. It is precisely these times that we must
rely on God and others to help us understand the motiva-
tions behind our behavior. This is why it is often helpful
to begin teaching children the cause and effect of their
behavior at an early age. School age children are capable
of understanding this over time. Why is he acting in an
irritable manner? Is he tired? Did he have a bad day at

school? Has someone or something disappointed him?

As parents, we must take the time to help a child see why he feels quarrelsome or irritable so that he can deal with the problem rather than placing blame upon others. Isaiah's message to Israel was to stop complaining and feeling confused. This Scripture goes on to say that the Lord does not grow weary and has no end to his understanding. It further states that he gives strength to the weary and hope for an answer so that we can renew our strength and soar on wings like eagles (40:27-31). Understanding, patience, and persistence can help our children learn from their mistakes as well.

Help Your Child Handle Life Hopefully. It has been observed that our children are being forced to grow up too soon. Our busy life-styles regularly cause our children to fend for themselves at an early age. Sometimes they simply do not have the resources and the emotional maturity to understand the changes going on around them. God gave children parents so they could remain children and learn to become adults gradually. Being fun-loving, free-spirited, and happy is a part of life that we owe them. It is important during this time that they develop hope, optimism, and high self-esteem to prepare them for the future. If we want to know how they view life, listen closely to the language they use, their enthusiasm for trying new experiences, and their attitudes.

Teenagers, perhaps, have more pressures on them in this generation than ever before. At a time when they are less accessible and more nonverbal, they need an opportunity to talk, try out new things, make mistakes, be unconditionally loved, and experience new freedom while being monitored closely. Teens often say no when they mean yes, are quiet when they want to talk, and push parents away when they need them to be close by. The following poem gives some insight into the need for optimism and hope in teenagers.

PLEASE HEAR WHAT I AM NOT SAYING

Don't be fooled by me.
Don't be fooled by the mask I wear.
For I wear a thousand masks.
Masks that I am afraid to take off, and none of them
  are me.
Pretending is an art that is second nature with me.
But don't be fooled by me.
For God's sake, don't be fooled.
I give the impression that I'm secure, that all is sunny
  and unruffled with me, within as well as without,
  that confidence is my name and I am in command,
  that I need no one.
But don't believe me . . . please!
It will not be easy for you.
A long conviction of worthlessness builds strong
  walls.
The nearer you approach me, the blinder I strike
  back.
I fight against the very thing I cry out for.
But I am told that love is stronger than walls, and
  in this lies my hope.
Please try to beat down those walls with a firm hand,
  but with gentle hands, for a child is very sensitive.
Who am I you might wonder?
I am someone you know very well, for I am every
  man you meet, and I am every woman you meet.

—Author Unknown

If parents are attuned to their children's negative comments, predictions of failure, critical remarks toward others, and gloomy attitudes, they can help them face the problems of growing up as they arise. God allows these to happen, according to Paul's words: "In all things God works for the good of those who love him, who have been called according to his purpose" (Rom. 8:28). Each new situation provides an opportunity to apply an effective solution. Finding the silver lining in every dark cloud is a skill that takes years of grooming and practice. Parents are responsible for equipping their children with this hopeful Christian attitude. There is a sign on the desk of a much-loved elder in our church that says, "Now let's talk about a few reasons why this can be done!" By refocusing on the possibilities instead of the problems, our children can learn to see opportunities in obstacles.

IGNORING AND ASKING FOR A CHANGE IN BEHAVIOR

When our oldest son was three years old, he got into a very unappealing habit of whining when he wanted something and did not get an immediate response. His whines were so grating upon our nerves that we found ourselves responding immediately to his demands in order to silence him. When we finally realized what we were encouraging in our son, we decided to take quick action. We sat him down and informed him that in the future when he did not talk like a "big boy," we would tell him that "I can't hear you" and go on about our business until he made his request in an acceptable tone. He would sometimes forget this agreement and revert back to his prior behavior until we stated, "I'm sorry, I can't hear you," upon which he would immediately change his tone and make his request in a more acceptable fashion.

There were times, however, when this did not work with him and we would have to ask him to go to his room until he could get happier. This would initially make the situation more unbearable, but he would usually comply. There were other times when he stood there in defiance refusing to do anything except make even more of a problem. At this, we would be forced to take him by the hand and walk him to his bedroom until he could compose himself and comply with our original arrangement. A problem that had existed for many months was solved in approximately one week with this approach.

As parents we sometimes forget how cherished our attention is to our children and how slight alterations of the above can make a world of difference to the atmosphere in the home. With older children, this can also work by asking them to "talk to me in a way that I can hear you."

FORCING A CHOICE BY EXAGGERATING THE OPTIONS

Almost every parent has had the unpleasant experience of trying to get a child in bed, have him brush his teeth, or have him eat the food on his plate. These are but a few of the daily ordeals that parents are forced to endure as young children learn to incorporate these responsibilities into their routine. Although children are dependent on their parents during the younger ages, they prefer to take on more responsibility as they get older. Unfortunately, these responsibilities may not be what is healthy for them. In preparing our children to come in to dinner or to get ready for bed, we often found ourselves with at least one uncooperative child unwilling to comply. We soon found that by giving them two choices, both of which were acceptable to us, our children were more likely to comply with a decision they themselves had made. For instance, when it was time to get ready for bed, we would ask, "Would you like to get ready to go to bed now or in five minutes?" Invariably, they would choose the latter, but it was their choice and one on which they very often followed through. If they didn't follow through on this, we would remind them that the following evening they would get ready when we chose for them to get ready.

One of the biggest challenges we ever met was getting our children to eat a new food they were sure they loathed, even though they had never tasted it. We would usually begin by placing at least a small serving of the abhorred substance on their plate so they could begin getting accustomed to it. While we usually made them only taste one forkful of the new food, they were presented a choice of eating the entire serving or just one bite. Being the astute children that they were, it did not take long to realize that one bite would secure them their freedom. If their tactics included waiting at the table until everyone else had finished and left in hopes that they would be forgotten, a five-minute timer was set. If they had not sampled the one forkful of food during the time limit, all of it would have to be eaten. This detoured a great number of arguments, allowed us all to win, and introduced them to a wide variety of different foods, many of which they now love.

This kind of intervention is limited only by one's imagination and can be used in a variety of situations. By giving a child a choice between being alone with his negativity or being with the rest of the family and having a good attitude, it is amazing how contented an initially disgruntled child can eventually become. In Numbers we read of how the Lord gave the Israelite people the choice of being happy with the food he had provided them or having so much they would be sick of it. In fact, he told the Israelites, "You will not eat it for just one day, or two days, or five, ten or twenty days, but for a whole month—until it comes out of your nostrils and you loathe it—because you have rejected the Lord, who is among you, and have wailed before him, saying, 'Why did we ever leave Egypt?' " (11:19-20).

SEPARATION OR ISOLATION

The Lord informed Moses that anyone who sinned defiantly would be cut off from his people (Num. 15:30). Sometimes unacceptable behavior can be remedied only by separating the offender from the rest of the family. This no longer gives the offender an audience toward whom he can voice his disgruntlement, and it allows him to be miserable by himself. "Time outs" serve the same purpose with children

when they are sent to their room to think over their misbehavior. Most people do not enjoy being alone for an
extended period of time, and isolation can often cause a
rather quick change of heart.

REMINDING THEM OF PAST CONSEQUENCES

It is amazing how quickly we forget those things that are
unpleasant to us. On occasions, it is helpful to be reminded
of just how painful a past experience was. God reminded
his people of this: "Only be careful, and watch yourselves
closely so that you do not forget the things your eyes have
seen or let them slip from your heart as long as you live.
Teach them to your children and to their children after
them" (Deut. 4:9). When we can be helped to recall the
inconvenience and discomfort of past consequences, it is
amusing to see how quickly our mind and emotions can
change.

ADDITIONAL CONSEQUENCES FOR
NONCOMPLIANCE

It can be very irritating for a parent to assign a consequence
for a child's behavior and realize no immediate change in
his response. Often a child will continue if he knows he is
upsetting the parent. To some children, this alone is worth
the consequences. In case of this type of "power play," it
is often helpful to give the child a choice that if this behavior
continues the consequences will be increased by small
increments. This gives the child control over the amount
of the consequence. A parent must describe this intervention in a neutral tone and give the child the choices without
acting angrily. If the parent can demonstrate a laissez-faire
or "it's your decision" attitude, the child often realizes that
the emotional pay-off has ended and they are only hurting
themselves.

This is by no means an exhaustive list of interventions

parents can use to curb arguing, complaining, or whining within their children. They should be used with care and caution, realizing that first and foremost is the well-being of the child. No technique is an answer alone but of utmost importance is the genuine care and concern we have for our child's well-being.

LYING AND DISHONESTY

"Truth decay" is one of the biggest concerns of parents today. More than anything, we would like to always believe our children are being honest with us. However, truthfulness is not an easy virtue to master as a child, and it takes years of practice and direction to understand its importance. To ensure that lying will not become a problem in our family, we need to help our children learn several important lessons.

First and foremost, they must know what lying is. Second, they must be taught to distinguish fact from fantasy. Third, they must have a deep respect and value for the truth. Finally, they must learn to use truth tactfully and speak the truth in love.

Lying involves all those deliberate violations of truth when truth is expected by the listener. In other words, there has been some intent in part or whole by the person to misinform, deceive, misrepresent, or omit.

What are the causes of lying or deceit? Children, at times, will exaggerate and fabricate stories in order to feel and look important to their peers. Some exaggeration is a normal part of fantasy life in children, although if it continues and becomes more and more excessive, some real problems may exist. For instance, some children will falsely report having made higher grades than they actually did. They may talk of having items at home that they really do not own, or of doing things that they really have not done to impress their friends.

Another reason children choose deceit instead of truthfulness is to escape punishment. They may be afraid of the consequences of telling the truth. For instance, recently in my office, I was seeing a family with an eight-year-old boy. After a while, I escorted him to the waiting room so I could talk with his parents alone. As I was returning to my office, I heard the receptionist's dial tone come on. Turning around, I observed my young client standing next to the receptionist's desk saying, "I didn't do it—it just came on by itself." Clearly, he anticipated some punishment for his inquisitiveness and sought immediately to protect himself. Trying to assure him that he was more important than the phones, yet at the same time encouraging truthfulness on his part, I said, "It's okay for you to touch the phones; they are interesting, aren't they?"

Emotional immaturity or feelings of inferiority can also contribute to children being untruthful. No one likes to feel worse about himself than he already does, and rather than admit a failure, sometimes a child will mislead. At times, there is more than one cause of lying, as when an individual is afraid of punishment and uses lying to blame someone else. This may save themselves and allow them to gain an advantage at the same time.

It is important to instill within children at a very young age how God views things. The writer of Proverbs said that there are six things the Lord hates, one of them being a "lying tongue" (6:16). Children are more apt to avoid lying and adhere to the truth when they know that God himself hates dishonesty.

FACT OR FANTASY

The need to distinguish fact from fantasy is universal. It is very difficult for young children to recognize the difference between something they have imagined and something that may have actually occurred. When watching TV, they may easily assume that what they are observing is in fact occurring. When children wake up from dreams, they often very strongly believe that those events did occur. While children can distinguish the basic meaning of some truths as early as three years old, their fantasy life does remain vivid through the ages of eight or nine and older. Sometimes even adults have to be careful not to close their eyes to reality. For instance, we may blame the wind for the direction our golf ball takes rather than admit it was the way we held our club, or we wear baggy clothing to cover excess bulges we wish were not there, and we even tell ourselves and everyone else present that we do not need this dessert, yet we sit there and consume it anyway.

Children need a fantasy life and the world of make-believe and pretend in order to develop their creativity as well as handle the harsh realities of life.

RESPECT FOR TRUTH

Adults often unwittingly teach their children that, at certain times, total honesty is not necessary. When we drive over the speed limit or only slow down for a stop sign, we are making a statement to our children about the importance of truthfulness. At those ages, they are watching very closely about how much we adhere to what we say. Learning to value truth is a difficult lesson for both parents and children. An essential is maintaining an open, accepting relationship between parents and children.

Parents must communicate by example to their children that their conviction for truth is strong. Being able to admit when we are wrong is essential. When children see their parents also wrestling with the issues of truthfulness, these children gain an increased appreciation of the value of that truth. Likewise, if parents make excuses for their behavior and accept "little white lies," the children have reason to doubt truth's importance. A parent who tells a child to inform a telephone caller that he is not home or is not available simply because the parent does not wish to speak with the caller is giving the child a very strong message about "situational ethics."

The child must also be helped to understand that truth has practical values. Actually, honesty saves time. A direct answer can save many minutes of confusion, justifying, or rationalizing. A straightforward tactful refusal of an invitation is much more honest than making excuses in order to save another person's feelings. Also, honesty builds trust, and relationships cannot exist or deepen without trust.

Most children have a need for approval from their parents. Children will do almost anything to avoid losing that approval, especially if they know their parents will back them up in any situation they find themselves. In my family, honesty was next to godliness. It did not matter what we did, but we always told the truth. When I was about seven years old, playing with a slingshot and a BB, I accidentally shot out the car window of my father's boss. I was pretending that his car was a monster and that it was attacking. I did not have the forethought to realize the damage it might cause. I still recall the temptation for just an instant to tell my father that I wasn't shooting at the car and just omit that vital piece of information. I knew, however, that if he ever found out, he would not trust me again. So, when he came home from his trip with the boss and saw the window, I told him the truth. To my surprise, he did not punish me except to make me pay for the cost of the window, and he appreciated my truthfulness in the matter. Without a doubt, this unexpected treatment by my father has been indelibly etched in my mind so that truth is also of the highest value in my family with our children.

INTERVENTIONS

One of the first things a family can begin doing is to establish truthfulness as a virtue more important than any other in the family next to love. Why is this? It is important for everyone to be able to trust each other, especially in the family. Honesty ensures the strong development of our character, our heart, and our identity. More than any other characteristic, honesty helps us become pure, blameless, holy, and Christ-like.

Second, we can help our children realize how serious lying is to God. Dishonesty anesthetizes our conscience, hampers our concern for others, separates us from each other, and especially hurts Jesus. It is also important to teach them that all lies will be found out and exposed. Matthew recorded Jesus' words:

> *Make a tree good and its fruit will be good, or make a tree bad and its fruit will be bad, for a tree is recognized by its fruit. . . . For out of the overflow of the heart the mouth speaks. The good man brings good things out of the good stored up in him, and the evil man brings evil things out of the evil stored up in him. But I tell you that men will have to give account on the day of judgment for every careless word they have spoken. For by your words you will be acquitted, and by your words you will be condemned. (12:33-37)*

Earlier in Matthew we read: "There is nothing concealed that will not be disclosed, or hidden that will not be made known" (10:26). This is quite a motivation for most people to deal with deceit on their own.

Third, as a parent, it is important to see the situation through the eyes of our children. They are continuing to develop their value systems as they mature, and these will be challenged by their exposure to radio, television, and other people. By standing in their shoes and understanding their perspective, we can assess our child's judgment, maturity level, and motives.

Next, children should be fully aware that premeditated lying is a major offense. If one is deliberately dishonest and deceitful, he should understand the consequences will be much worse. Dishonesty has such long-reaching effects, it cannot be treated lightly.

Fifth, reassure your child that truthfulness is much more important to you than what they may have done wrong. Years ago, a man's word was his honor. It was more important for him to be dependable and reliable in what he said than anything else. It is often helpful to give a child time to think it over if you suspect he is not telling the truth. Untruths are often said quickly under pressure and without forethought. If someone else was lied to or lied about, our child should be made to right that wrong and apologize in person to the other individuals involved.

Next, parents who tactfully confirm what they have been told by their children through reliable sources can build a deeper trust in their child's honesty. It is worthwhile to do spot checks or intermittently follow up on what you as a parent have been told by your child. This gives the parent the freedom to monitor his child on occasion and allows the child to realize his parent has the freedom and the concern to do that.

There are any number of consequences that are appropriate for dishonesty including isolation, grounding, withdrawal of privileges, spanking, writing sentences, or library reports on honesty. These, of course, are based on the extent of the offenses.

Last, if more than one child is involved in a conspiracy, it is often helpful to separate them to hear their stories apart from one another. This allows the parents the freedom to check on inconsistencies without wondering if their child can be trusted.

These are just a few of the interventions that can be used with a child that has had problems telling the truth. Each child is different, and each situation has many alternatives available to it.

THE SILENT TREATMENT

America's number one form of emotional warfare is the silent treatment. If for whatever reason we do not like someone, it is easiest just to ignore him or to act as if he does not exist. Adults have been doing this to one another for years, and perhaps this is why teenagers use the silent treatment so effectively. Teenagers use the silent treatment when they are angry at someone, when they are afraid, or when they are attempting to protect themselves. Silence often helps them to avoid an existing conflict, at least for the present. Queen Esther was faced with the dilemma of remaining silent and possibly saving her own life or speaking out and saving the lives of the people of Israel from Haman's plans.

Silence may mean we feel so emotionally overwhelmed that we are at a loss for words. Such silence indicates a sense of anxiety or apprehension, implying feelings of hopelessness or inadequacy rather than an attempt to willfully withhold anything. When silence is used to manipulate others into doing what we want them to do, or in an effort to coerce them to give in to our demands, it is clearly an unfair weapon.

At times a teenager may try to punish his parents by excluding them. This behavior is sometimes known as passive aggression. It is easily defended by maintaining that "nothing is wrong" while the attitude of resentment is very obvious.

INTERVENTIONS INTO THE SILENT TREATMENT

When a normally talkative, rambunctious child or teenager becomes more reserved or quiet, there is usually a reason. He or she may either be tired, sick, moody, disappointed, daydreaming, hurt, or angry. When your child is silent because of hurt or anger, it is important to investigate the causes of this emotional state. If his or her condition is a result of a disagreement between the two of you, it is likely that you are being faced with a case of oppositional behavior.

To begin with, it is more profitable to combat silence with love and goodness. Scripture counsels, " 'If your enemy is hungry, feed him; if he is thirsty, give him something to drink. In doing this, you will heap burning coals on his head.' Do not be overcome by evil, but overcome evil with good" (Rom. 12:20). It takes two to tangle, and if your mood is not ruffled by your child's attempts to incite you, the fuel for his fire will quickly burn out.

If this approach is not enough to turn the tide, warnings of the impending punishment can help them think over their behavior and perhaps change it. The Lord showed Amos a basket of ripe fruit and said, " 'The time is ripe for my people Israel; I will spare them no longer. In that day,' declares the Sovereign Lord, 'the songs in the temple will turn to wailing' " (Amos 8:2). This offers children a choice to continue acting in the same way with a guarantee of impending consequences or to change their behavior and avoid them.

Still another approach to dealing with the silent treatment is to add consequences at different increments of time with the promise of more consequences the longer they maintain their mood. This allows them to have control over how much worse they want the situation to become. A period of isolation or time out is helpful and is all that is needed for most children. However, more drastic measures are occasionally necessary. In an effort to break the silence, parents can also ask questions that only require a yes or no answer. If children will begin answering these questions, they are generally on the road to talking more.

If these efforts do not soften their resistance, reverse psychology that restrains them from saying too much because of the "mess" they would probably make of the situation often entices participation.

After discouraging the silent child from speaking for his own good, then continue talking about the seriousness of this problem to the other family members in the room. By purposefully misrepresenting the silent child's motives, he will have to correct you, and therefore begin speaking. This should not be done in a derogatory or hurtful manner, but in an inquisitive, matter-of-fact way that suggests you as a parent are interested in understanding what is behind this behavior.

The attitude of "I wonder what's going on here?" is one of the best ways to encourage the silent teenager's participation. Blame and criticism should be avoided, and a genuine interest is best communicated to the third party in order to motivate the silent party's participation. Sometimes asking one sibling about the other sibling's motives is enough to incite the silent sibling into talking for himself. A parent, however, must be careful not to create another problem between the silent teenager and his brother or sister.

When the silent treatment has been used to punish and manipulate parents, and the above interventions have been ineffective, a combination of two approaches can be helpful. The parents can isolate children in their room and give them permission to remain silent. The reason for isolating them is to take advantage of the power in weakness. When a parent cannot make his child feel better, the child is, in effect, in control. He defeats his parents by not allowing them to change his mood or attitude. By isolating him and giving him permission to feel bad the child is rendered powerless.

This prescription should be presented in a kind, concerned, and benign way without frustration or a vindictive tone. For instance, a parent could tell his child, "Perhaps it would be best for you to sit here by yourself and think about how miserable things are. Sometimes we do have to feel worse before we can feel better." The attitude that was at first the child's weapon against his parents now becomes his parents' suggestion for him to remain that way and is therefore no longer his own idea. A change in attitude usually occurs in a very short time when this kind of intervention is correctly used.

Be careful in using some of these latter interventions because if not handled correctly the situation may be worsened. Try some of the simpler suggestions first. Of course, no matter what intervention is used to neutralize this problem, it is always important to sit down and talk with the children about what caused their concerns. Anger, resentment, and pride are problems we must all deal with, and these suggestions are merely some ways to break the ice so that this process can begin. Some of these ideas may seem revolutionary and somewhat radical in comparison to traditional approaches to childrearing, but they are intended to be a means to an end.

CONCLUSION

An insightful little poem was written a number of years ago by Dorothy Law Nolte:

> *Children Learn What They Live*
>
> *If a child lives with criticism, he learns to condemn;*
> *If a child lives with hostility, he learns to fight;*
> *If a child lives with ridicule, he learns to be shy;*
> *If a child lives with shame, he learns to feel guilty;*
> *If a child lives with tolerance, he learns to be patient;*
> *If a child lives with encouragement, he learns*
>   *confidence;*
> *If a child lives with praise, he learns to appreciate;*
> *If a child lives with fairness, he learns justice;*
> *If a child lives with security, he learns to have faith;*
> *If a child lives with approval, he learns to like*
>   *himself;*
> *If a child lives with acceptance and friendship, he*
>   *learns to find love in the world.*

Consider these additional lines that might summarize what this chapter can mean to a child:

If a child lives with arguing, he learns to be negative;
If a child lives with firm fairness, he learns cooperation;
If a child lives with dishonesty, he learns how to deceive;
If a child lives with truthfulness, he learns how to succeed;
If a child lives with silence, he learns to resent;
If a child lives with dialogue, he learns to resolve;
If a child lives with God's love, he learns to give God's love.

5
School Problems
Kent R. Brand, A.C.S.W.

One of the most distressing problems for parents is to receive a negative conduct or progress report from the school concerning their child. A parent in this situation may feel embarrassment, anger, disappointment, anxiety, or a sense of personal failure.

After regularly receiving glowing reports from the school regarding our first two children, Becky and I were very concerned when we received word from the school that our third child was having some academic and behavior problems.

I had always thought that being a minister and a counselor would exempt us from such problems. Having counseled with hundreds of parents of children with school problems, I was able to humble myself before God and receive some of my own advice. After much prayer, interaction with the teacher, and individual help for our son at home, I was later pleased and relieved when he began receiving outstanding school marks. His behavior also improved and he received several "Citizen of the Month" awards.

There is hope for parents whose children are having

difficulties in school. We must keep in mind that God has created each child with different abilities and different personalities. Therefore, some children will be able to achieve higher academic results than others. However, with God's help, each child can learn to be a success and to do his best in his school work.

Each year on the first day of school, our family devotional is centered around the life of Daniel. Daniel was a man of excellence, who was chosen to serve Nebuchadnezzar, king of Babylon. He was a man who showed aptitude for every kind of learning, was well informed, quick to understand, and qualified to serve in the king's palace. He was to be educated for three years and then entered in the king's service. Because of Daniel's faith, God gave him knowledge and understanding of all kinds of literature and learning. In fact, Daniel and his godly friends were found to be ten times better than all the magicians and enchanters of Nebuchadnezzar's kingdom (Dan. 1).

Our lesson to our children from this story is that God expects us to strive for excellence. He wants us to work hard and to trust in him for success and guidance. It is my conviction that children who learn to discipline themselves well in school will be able to discipline themselves in their job, marriage, and the Lord's kingdom as adults. Learning to be a success at school is a great foundation for future success and fruitfulness in God's kingdom.

CAUSES OF SCHOOL PROBLEMS

After counseling hundreds of families whose children have had school difficulties, I have found that the failure to establish team effort, with both parents and teachers cooperating, is a primary cause of school problems. Whenever I am called for consultation regarding school problems with a child, I request a joint meeting with the parents, teachers, and the child. Just calling this meeting often alters the attitude of a child who has not given his full effort. If parents have been remiss in providing adequate monitoring of their child's progress, such a meeting can address this problem also. Clarifying what each individual's role is in the process can be an extremely effective method of dealing with school problems.

Many times, school problems can be solved by the parents and teachers remaining in close contact and meeting on a regular basis. The fact that the child knows the parents and teachers are communicating has a great impact on the child's behavior. When this basic principle is practiced, I have seen many problems disappear. If the problem persists, then the family may need to seek ongoing counseling.

There are many ways for parents to be involved in their child's school activities. I often have lunch with my children at school. At least once a year, I can also observe the teacher's classroom in action. Of course, there is the P.T.A., school programs, and other ways of being involved in school activities. Becky, my wife, has often volunteered to help out with the classroom, sell refreshments at special school functions, or assist the teacher as projects arise. When the teacher has a parent who is interested in being involved at school, the teacher often has a more positive attitude toward the child. Just this change in the teacher's attitude alone can often result in great changes in a child.

One of the great advantages of a "team meeting" between parents and teachers is that the child receives consistent input at school and at home. When the child sees the parents and teachers cooperating, it gives him a greater respect for authority and, therefore, behavior and attitudes will most likely improve.

COMMON PROBLEMS

Disrespect. Disrespect for authority is one of the most common problems that teachers face. Children receive many messages from the media and from their peers that seem to encourage the attitude: "You can't make me." Often parents and teachers become bewildered and frustrated by this mentality. This is why it is helpful to decide on an effective way of bringing this type of child under control. Responses that rarely work and only bring temporary relief include ignoring the behavior and hoping it will disappear, extensive reasoning with the child, angrily reacting toward the behavior, or resignation.

The power structure in the classroom and at home must be clearly restored if a child is defying authority. Outlining specific expectations about positive behaviors and setting limitations on the negative behaviors of a child can be best accomplished at a neutral time instead of in the midst of a conflict. By understanding what the rewards for desired behavior and consequences for unacceptable behavior are, the child can be reminded of the prior arrangement and head off many regressions. This action places control of the child's behavior in his own hands because of the choices that have been made available to him. Parents need not become angry or punitive when an offense has occurred, but need only to follow through with what was previously decided.

If this is not effective, a more direct, serious approach may be necessary to address open rebellion. Yet it must be administered with dignity, without a show of anger, and with genuine concern for the welfare of the child. "Do not withhold discipline from a child; if you punish him with the rod, he will not die. Punish him with the rod and save his soul from death" (Prov. 23:13-14). "The rod of correction imparts wisdom, but a child left to himself disgraces his mother" (Prov. 29:15).

The parent and teacher must decide on an effective way of bringing this child under control.

Anxiety. Another common problem for children in school is anxiety. Nervousness can stem from unfamiliarity with a new situation, insecurity, shyness, fear of failure, previous traumas, family problems, divorce, or abuse. Parents and teachers need to determine if a child's apprehensiveness is merely a normal reaction to new surroundings that lessens with time and exposure or if the degree and duration are serious enough to warrant concern and special attention. High levels of anxiety can confuse the child and diminish his ability to concentrate. A family in this situation may need to seek Christian family therapy immediately. The problem will often improve more expediently with the whole family involved.

Children will also worry about peer relationships or scenes that they see on television. Family devotionals that ask the question, "What are some of your worries?" can be a part of the parents' strategy. Such questions will encourage communication about anxieties and fears that come even from outside of the family.

I can remember the day my oldest child started kindergarten. He expressed his fear about going to school. We stopped, talked, prayed about it, and he felt more confident in facing his first day. Now he is fifteen years old, and God has certainly given him many victories in school. He is consistently on the honor roll and was a starter for his junior varsity basketball team this year.

Learning Disorders. Learning disorders are another common but often unrecognized problem for children in school. These problems need to be professionally diagnosed. Some of the causes of learning disorders are: (1) developmental trauma, (2) an inherited disability, (3) allergies, (4) cerebral dysfunction, (5) improper supervision, or (6) improper school placement.

An evaluation for learning disorders may be needed if your child exhibits symptoms such as: (1) a reading level two years below his grade level, (2) excessive problems with attention and listening, (3) hyperactive or hyperkinetic behavior, (4) dyslexia (substantial reversal and misplacement of letters and numbers), or (5) poor memory or retention of learned material. The evaluation may include educational or psychological tests, hearing tests, or vision tests to rule out certain possibilities.

There will be different prescriptions for different problems. Diagnosis from a professional trained in the area of learning disorders is imperative. Excellent planning with the school is also essential. Parents and teachers need to give the child a great deal of patience and reinforcement for any progress. Reinforcement by praise is extremely crucial. This child may also need very basic help in improving study skills, organization, and discipline.

Anger and Aggression. Angry outbursts and aggression are often problems for children in school. We realize that TV and society place a great deal of emphasis on assertiveness, power, control, and being "macho." Parents and teachers must not allow a child to intimidate other children with aggression. Intervention must be quick and effective.

Often a child who fights frequently is insecure, frightened, or angry about problems at home. This child needs to be taught appropriate and constructive ways to channel his aggression in order to build his self-esteem. Sports is one vehicle. Several years ago, we had a problem with one of our children in this area. My wife taught this child a memory verse from Proverbs 16:32: "Better a patient man than a warrior, a man who controls his temper than one who takes a city."

A child who experiences temper outbursts often is very sensitive, feels things deeply, and has the potential for strong values. By praying with the child and talking through his feelings, the child can learn to channel his frustrations at school in a positive direction. When trying to be understanding, talking to the child, and allowing him to express his needs do not change the problem, limits should be placed upon unacceptable behavior. If the child does not control himself, he needs to suffer the consequences.

If angry outbursts persist, counseling for the family may

be indicated to discover how they handle stress, frustrations, and daily difficulties as a unit.

The Victim. There is also the problem of the child being the victim of others' misbehavior at school. These problems need to be brought to the teacher's and principal's attention immediately. The child who is aggressive needs to be restrained, and the child who is being victimized needs to be protected. In addition, the child who is being mistreated by his peers needs to learn coping mechanisms to be able to overcome the difficulty. For instance, when I was counseling at the mental health clinic in graduate school, I saw an elementary school child whose initials were R.C. Many children at school called him "R.C. Cola." This nickname infuriated the young man and caused an extreme reaction by him. By simply teaching him to ignore this behavior, he was able to gain control of the situation and hence have more power over those who were teasing him.

Attention Seekers. Another common school problem is the attention seeker. Dr. James Dobson in his book, *Dr. Dobson Answers Your Questions,*[1] states that he handled this issue as a teacher by sending a child to an isolated part of the room where the child could not be seen by other students. In severe cases, he would send the child to an isolated part of the room for as long as a week at a time. This method was important in bringing the child's classroom behavior under control.

The parents of an attention seeker must ask themselves the questions, "Am I spending enough time with my child?" Chances are that the child has been overlooked and feels somewhat neglected. The attention-seeking behavior is simply masking feelings of inadequacy. This child needs reinforcement of positive behavior by praise and other rewarding mechanisms. In addition, this child can be given classroom responsibilities that will give him a legitimate way of getting attention from other classmates.

The Bored Child. Some children are "turned off" or "tuned out." They are bored and undermotivated. Sometimes the classroom learning can be too easy or too difficult. In addition, there may be problems at home that preoccupy the child's thoughts. The parents and teachers must think of more creative ways for this child to learn. Parents should take the child to the library, go on field trips, and help the child get answers to a lot of "why" questions about life. Parents can pray with the child about completing his work and having an exciting day. To a child who experiences boredom, a parent's parting words should be, "I love you," and, "See what new thing you can learn today." Parents' prayers for a bored child should include the opportunity for the child to experience leadership, rewards for success-es, and special attention from the teacher.

A lot of time and attention by both the teacher and parent needs to be given to the child. Sometimes the expectations need to be reduced, and sometimes they need to be in-creased. The parent or teacher may also write out a contract in which the child agrees to explore some exciting new discoveries. Albert Einstein's lack of early academic success should encourage parents that this problem can be over-come in a great and victorious way.

School Phobia. School phobia is not so frequent a problem, but it can be quite severe when experienced. This problem cannot be ignored but should be handled immediately. The reason for the school phobia must first of all be evaluated. Sometimes children are trying to protect a parent or feel they cannot leave them alone at home. Sometimes expec-tations are too high at school, and the child is afraid to fail. Occasionally the child has had a traumatic experience or another child is threatening him.

First of all, the child should see that his total environment is concerned and willing to help out. A meeting must be called of all significant people in the child's life. This will get the child's attention and see how important this prob-lem is.

The parents should then begin teaching earnestly about how to deal with fears. The story of Jonah from God's Word should be explored in depth. The child should see dramatically what happened when Jonah ran away from his responsibilities. In addition, a contract should be set up between the child and parent in which the child receives positive rewards for each day of attendance at school. By the child having something positive to work for, the powerful desire for reward will eventually overcome the fears. If the problem originates in a dependent, protective relationship between child and parent, family therapy is almost always recommended.

SUCCESSFUL STRATEGIES IN OTHER SCHOOL ISSUES

Contracts. One method of intervention that I have found extremely successful with elementary children between the ages of five and twelve is a school contract (see Appendix) involving parent, teacher, counselor, and child. The method of the contract should be carefully explained to each person involved. The idea is that the child chooses some reward or activity of value to him. A list of approximately five to ten desired items is usually sufficient. Then, a total point value can be ascribed to each individual toy or activity. For instance, an ice cream cone might be worth fifty points, a kite might be worth two hundred points, a doll might be worth twelve hundred points, or a Monopoly game, eight hundred points. Then the child chooses one or more problems that he will work on for a week. The more difficult the problem, the higher the value of points. The easier problems receive a lower value of points. The child receives points each day for success in overcoming the problem.

The child is then asked to make a strong commitment to working hard on the contract. The child is asked to sign the contract. Then the child takes the contract to school. The teacher will initial each day that the child is successfully victorious over each problem. At the end of the week, the child will bring the contract either to the counselor or to the parent. The total number of points can be tallied, and the number of points can either be used for a reward or saved for a future goal. The parent or counselor should also discuss ways to improve for the next week. Then the child is able to choose either the same or new problems for the new contract.

The same procedure is repeated until the child is victorious over all the identified problems. A celebration party including parents, teacher, child, and counselor can then follow. At this point, the child can be removed from the contract. Parents will need to continue to reinforce good behavior with praise, encouragement, and physical affection.

Meeting Needs Outside of School. Parents must also be sure that the basic needs of their children have been met before the child leaves for school. Sometimes, teachers see children who are too sleepy, hungry, or inappropriately dressed at school. Make sure that your child has an early bedtime. Except for nights when we have church activities, our school-aged children are in bed by 8:00 P.M. When there is a church activity that will keep the children up a little later, the children will often take a nap. Also making sure that children are physically and spiritually fed before they leave for school insures them that they will have a bright, positive, cheerful outlook on the day.

Since some children are very hard on clothes, it is important for parents to frequently take a look at the child's wardrobe to make sure his clothes are adequately intact and in fashion. This will remove one more obstacle by keeping him from unnecessary ridicule.

Another key issue is for parents to help the child be appropriate for school in dress, preparation for gym, and having appropriate hygiene. If these details are not taken care of, they can cause embarrassment for the child, causing him to fall into disfavor with the teacher and other students.

The parents also need to be very concerned about providing an environment that facilitates completed homework. Children need to have an area of the house where they can concentrate and be alone. It is also important for preschool children to have areas of the home where they can develop concentration and organized thinking.

If all the previous methods fail, and you feel that the professional teachers involved are neglecting or misjudging your child, you need to go to the higher authorities in defense of your child. Do not sit idle. Be active and defend the rights of your child to have an excellent education.

TEENS AND PARENTAL INFLUENCE

Often, parents will do an excellent job of being involved in the school while their child is in elementary school. However, when the child enters middle school and high school, the parents often make the drastic mistake of withdrawing. The child then needs you more than ever, especially during the crucial early-teen years. Of course, the school involvement will take on a different form, but it should still be there. Since peers have such a strong influence during the teen years, the parents often withdraw and say, "I have no further influence over the child." Again, this is a drastic mistake. A survey completed in Minnesota of 8,000 teenagers showed that parents were still the number-one influence in a child's life during the adolescent years. This is in spite of strong peer relationships and interaction.

TELEVISION

Not all TV is bad, but too much TV can have a negative effect upon children's school performance. The scriptural principle that "whatever a man thinks in his heart, he will become" is certainly true of the TV input children receive today. In March, 1985, the Associated Press pointed out that the American Psychological Association has taken a position on the potential dangers in television violence. Also, the American Academy of Pediatrics released in *USA Today* the fact that repeated exposure to TV violence can make children not only accepting of real-life violence but more violent themselves. Zig Ziglar says in his book *Raising Positive Kids in a Negative World*: "When your child is in front of a television set or movie screen, you are permitting him to be educated (indoctrinated) by the most effective and persuasive tool in America today."[2]

Every hour that a child invests in television is one less hour that is invested in personal motivation, mental creativity, and actual involvement in the lives of others. In our family, we have a rule that there is to be no more than three hours of television per week.

A school in Pennsylvania has drawn up guidelines setting strict limits of watching television in an effort to rid students of hyperactivity, nervousness, and antisocial behavior. Children in the second grade and above are urged to avoid TV on school nights and to restrict weekend viewing to no more than three or four hours. The effects of this are easily observable. The children concentrate better and are more able to follow directions and get along better with their fellow students. If the children go back to the TV set, you notice the difference immediately.

One recent development that can help parents in monitoring what is seen on TV is the use of the video recorder. The parents must be careful in choosing programs that would be inspiring, uplifting, and supporting Christian values.

MORALS

Because strong moral values are not currently taught as much in the school system as in past years, children will have a tendency to relate negative values they are learning in school to real life. For this reason and because of God's admonitions, I strongly urge each Christian family to be constantly teaching God's values to their children.

Whenever I hear that sex education is going to be taught at school, I arrange family devotionals on sex for at least a week or two. Some of the various topics include the warnings from Proverbs, the glories of sex in marriage, and practical examples like Joseph.

Children need to be taught God's values about relationships, which schools only rarely teach. Learning God's values is crucial to spiritual and social development. Family devotional topics can include being a servant, how to choose friends, how to resolve conflict, what to do with jealous feelings, and many other relationship topics. Unhealthy values that are promoted in school should be evaluated during the family devotionals. "A wise man attacks the city of the mighty and pulls down the stronghold in which they trust" (Prov. 21:22). Any evil or ungodly teaching should be exposed in this way.

WISDOM

Some schooling issues should be left up to each individual parent's wisdom and trust in God. The issues of home school versus public school, or public school versus Christian school fall into the category of Romans 14. We should accept one another's decisions in these areas without passing judgment on one another. "Let us therefore make every effort to do what leads to peace and mutual edification" (Rom. 14:19). Christians who send their children to public schools, Christian schools, or teach their children at home, should not judge one another regarding whether this is right or wrong in God's sight.

Parents need to totally trust God for his wisdom and direction for their children. There are advantages and disadvantages of each of the three forms of education listed above. However, God can make it clear which form of education is best for your child.

"I have told you these things so that in me you may have peace. In this world you will have trouble, but take heart! I have overcome the world" (John 16:33). Those who seek to follow Jesus Christ are not immune to school problems. However, by a deep trust in God and a strong prayer life, we can have confidence that God will give us great victories for our children in their education. In addition, we need to pray that they will use their profession to glorify God and be abundantly fruitful in his kingdom.

6

The Shy Child
Samuel D. Laing

We have all seen them. Perhaps we have been one—the shy child. Withdrawn, quiet, shrinking from new people and new situations, they never seem to be comfortable unless they are alone or unless they are in a totally "safe" zone. We worry about them. We pity them. Or we are *determined* to change them!

Parents have come to the point of divorce trying to agree on how to raise them. Are shy children victims or manipulators? Is it the parents' fault? What did they do wrong?

Let us understand right away that some children are quieter and more reserved than others. And that is good. Not everyone needs to be a super-extrovert. We need some quiet, reflective, gentle people on this troubled planet. We should accept our child's basic personality as God's gift. But we should *not accept* withdrawal from others and from life due to fear, insecurity, or selfishness.

This chapter will not pretend to be a thorough study of all the reasons why a child is shy. But we will give those parents who have such a child some things to do right now to equip you to do a better job. It is possible, by instilling a deep faith in God and by encouraging the imitation of Christ, to bring about a wonderful growth in your child's personality and assertiveness. And that's what being a parent is all about.

STRATEGY #1: GIVE THEM YOUR LOVE AND NURTURE

Nothing is more important to a child's self-esteem and confidence, especially in the early formative years, than the knowledge of his or her parents' love and acceptance. This is an especially urgent need for those children who tend to lack confidence. Surround the shy child with love. Lavish praise upon him for every good deed. Reveal to him the good parts of his personality and character. Speak about him or her with godly pride in front of siblings, playmates, and family friends. Let him never justifiably doubt your love. And remember, this affirmation needs to be a daily, ongoing experience.

Sometimes we think our "quiet one" is less needful of love than his demanding, complaining, or rebellious sibling. Absolutely not true! Silent cooperation does not necessarily mean a child is secure or confident. Compliant children need your love just as much as the others. They may not leave that impression or know how to ask—but they need your love. Find the ways your love registers with your shy one and go with it. Affection, play, time, talk, whatever it takes—nurture this more fragile person into confidence.

> *People were bringing little children to Jesus to have him touch them, but the disciples rebuked them. When Jesus saw this, he was indignant. He said to them, "Let the little children come to me, and do not hinder them, for the kingdom of God belongs to such as these. I tell you the truth, anyone who will not receive the kingdom of God like a little child will never enter it." And he took the children in his arms,*

put his hands on them and blessed them. (Mark 10:13-16)

STRATEGY #2: GIVE THEM YOUR TIME

Love, especially to younger children, is equated to the time you give them. And, for shy children, greater amounts of time together are essential because in any situation it takes them longer to adjust and feel at ease. Some people go tromping through the woods and never see any wildlife. "There's nothing here," they think. Others go to the same forest, sit quietly in one spot, and find their patience rewarded with the presence and beauty of "all creatures great and small." It was there all along. But the reward is given to the patient. So it is in dealing with shy children.

Find those settings and subjects that draw out the more gentle, quieter child, and invest your time in these. The child may begin to reveal himself to you naturally, and you will be rewarded by a beautifully bonded friendship that lasts a lifetime.

STRATEGY #3: BE OPTIMISTIC
ABOUT THEIR CAPACITY FOR GROWTH

The fact that a child may have tendencies to shyness does not preclude the possibility of growth. Children can and do change. Sometimes the changes may come so quickly and rapidly as to dumbfound you. Other children may gradually, surely, gain in confidence and assertiveness over time. Do not be discouraged. Especially do not reveal any sense of defeat or frustration to your young pupil. If children sense this within you, they could interpret it in a fatalistic manner, causing them to lose heart and lapse into deeper withdrawal. A shy child must know that you love and accept him as he is even though he has some behaviors you want to help him to change. If you remain buoyant, hopeful, and optimistic, you will find your efforts will meet with greater success. Parents must learn to trust in the power of God in prayer and also remember that some things will be more easily overcome after the child becomes a Christian.

STRATEGY #4: PUSH THEM AHEAD GENTLY IN THEIR AREAS OF FEAR

Shy children often fear certain situations or certain activities to a marked degree. Fear is not necessarily bad. It is a God-given protective device. What must be overcome is a mentality of fearfulness or an inhibiting fearfulness. Gently encourage and urge shy children ahead when you spot an area of reticence. Use your judgment—not too much too soon. But keep them moving ahead. Praise and reward them for every conquest. The good feelings they derive about their newfound prowess will encourage them to be even more venturesome next time. Celebrate and savor the victory, give them time to solidify their gains, and then move forward again.

Do not be afraid to start with something small. Remember, size is a comparative value and is determined in the mind of your child. Every small achievement is a building block and will give you a "bank account" of encouraging memories with which to reassure your child in the midst of the next challenge. Do not humiliate a shy child by assigning some difficult deed in a highly public atmosphere. Privately prepare him well in advance for these occasions so that there is little chance for failure.

STRATEGY #5: ENCOURAGE UPBUILDING RELATIONSHIPS

Observe the shy child in his interactions with siblings and playmates. Inquire of his teachers about his relationships at day care or school. Watch, listen, and learn. Is there an ongoing relationship with a peer or peer group that is eroding your child's confidence? Are older, quick-witted siblings always interrupting and giving the answer first? Is the younger, cute child always getting the attention? Is there a more aggressive playmate continually dominating your child or making fun of his mistakes? If so, take corrective action. If possible, talk to the more dominant child and encourage a new attitude.

Discuss with the teacher what needs to be done. Diminish, discourage, or discontinue any relationship that is seriously undermining your child's ability to grow. A word of warning: Do not be overprotective. Teach your child to handle tough kids and tough situations. Teach him to be loving, but not to always give in just to have peace. Jesus was loving, but he stood up for what was right and was not afraid to challenge selfishness in others.

No doubt about it—this will take wisdom, advice, and trial and error, but do your best.

STRATEGY #6: GIVE THEM A CHANCE TO TALK IN FAMILY SETTINGS

Quieter children often have a lot to offer, but never have a chance to offer it. Around the dinner table, riding in the car, at family devotionals—they are shouted down and crowded out by the chatter of their more aggressive family members. Do not assume they are not thinking. Do not assume they do not care. Their silence may be caused by feeling that no one *wants* to listen. Maybe they have a tendency to mental and verbal laziness that needs to be deliberately countered by being asked to participate. Perhaps there is even a residual anger and frustration at always being preempted.

The solution? Give the shy child a chance to talk. Silence the boisterous siblings (or parent) and make them listen as the words come out, softly and slowly. At our home we have given our youngest the authority to raise his hand in a "V for Victory" sign to obtain the floor whenever he wishes. Call on the shy child in family devotionals. Seize upon anything close to being right or relevant in his comments, praise it, and you will see his words take on an increasing air of authority as his confidence grows.

STRATEGY #7: SEARCH YOUR OWN BEHAVIOR

We must be willing to look at ourselves as parents and see if we are contributing to our child's withdrawal. Here is a checklist:

Am I overprotective? Do I seek to shield my child from all pain, conflict, and difficulty? Do I rush to his defense in every altercation? Do I allow her to shrink back from needed challenges? Do I fear too much for his physical safety? Pain, defeat, and a certain degree of anxiety are a part of God's discipline that produces character. Let your child experience life.

Am I fearful myself? If you express your fears freely in front of your child, you will unwittingly make his or her problems worse. We need to guard against even the innocent expressions of concern that could be easily misinterpreted by a sensitive child. Build faith, not fear, into your children.

Do I use my child as a refuge from others? Some parents create a closed atmosphere in their home, using their children selfishly as a buffer against others. Children sense this fortress mentality and will withdraw even more to protect a weak parent from the world "out there."

Am I too pushy? If you push your child too hard athletically, socially, or academically, you will not help him gain confidence. Confidence must be built up, not snatched up. If we are too pushy, we should ask ourselves if we are either trying to live our life through our child, or if we lack the loving, patient understanding to work with a more sensitive personality. (One special note: If your child is barely the age to begin the school experience, be sure that there is adequate emotional and mental readiness. In my judgment, it is better to hold him back a year than to have him always laboring to keep up.)

Is there strain between me and my spouse? Continual arguments and bickering between parents only makes a sensitive child more fearful. Even if a child thinks there are problems between Mom and Dad, it will have negative results. Disagreements over how to treat a shy child should be worked out in private so that a united front can be presented.

STRATEGY #8: ENCOURAGE DEVELOPMENT OF AN AREA OF SKILL

Everyone has something they are good at and that they like doing. For the child who feels a sense of inadequacy, there can be an incredible transformation when a compensatory skill is attained in some worthy area. Whether it be music, academics, the arts, or athletics, encourage your child to develop at least one area of genuine competence. Make the time and situations available for this to happen. As a parent, take a genuine concern in *his or her* interests, even if they are very different from your own.

A Word of Warning: This skill or hobby should not be allowed to become a consuming fixation, nor should it be emphasized to the compromise of spiritual values. Parents who allow their children to become committed to organized sports to the point of missing church events are making a grievous error. These activities should be just activities—and no more. Confidence may be augmented by, but not built upon, special skills.

STRATEGY #9: ENCOURAGE LOVE
AND CONCERN FOR OTHERS

Shyness can be a sign of too much focus on oneself. The cure? Focus on others. Let their sensitive nature become a strength. Teach them to turn their sensitivity in an outward direction. Train them in the golden rule: "In everything, do to others what you would have them do to you" (Matt. 7:12).

Do not allow a shy child to feel that everyone else is wrong and that he should be treated with "kid gloves." If a child withdraws and is pitied and allowed to be sullen, selfish, and brooding, then he will have a life of misery. Draw him out. Urge him to become expressive of his love. Teach him to say thank you, hello, and to ask how *other* people are feeling. The best cure for an overprotective attitude toward self is a greater love for others. "Do not be overcome by evil, but overcome evil with good" (Rom. 12:21).

STRATEGY #10: LET THEM BE
OPEN WITH YOU IN PRIVATE

Time spent alone with a parent in open conversation is a must for withdrawn children. Talk to them. Tell them about your childhood. Identify with wide-ranging subjects. Discover their likes and dislikes, good feelings and bad feelings. Let them get to know you as a person.

Ask if he or she feels bad about anything. You may discover areas of guilt that need to be resolved. There may be some misdeed that has been covered over and remains for him or her a source of dread and fear. If you note a marked swing in mood, draw the child aside and, in a private setting, gently seek to uncover the source. It may be easily resolved, or it may be an area that will require further discussion, prayer, and Bible study. There may have been an incident of physical or sexual abuse that needs to come into the open. There may simply be doubts and questions that need to be brought into the healing light. Whatever the case, cultivate a genuine, honest, and open relationship so that *you* know your child and he or she knows you.

STRATEGY #11: ENCOURAGE CONTACT WITH OTHERS

This may seem a simple strategy, but we often overlook the obvious. By this we mean involving your child with individual playmates—and with groups of other children. Shy children simply must be exposed to the give-and-take world. To pull them away or allow them to withdraw too much is unrealistic and harmful.

Here is where the advantage of strong Christian fellowship reveals itself. Encourage friendships with other adults or "big brothers" or "big sisters." Allow and urge these folks to take your child for short periods of time. Encourage them to do special things together and to join with other families in their activities. This allows your child to develop social confidence on his own, not becoming overly-dependent on your presence. It also allows a less sociable child to grow in his interactive skills in an environment you know to be safe.

STRATEGY #12: TEACH THEM THE UNCONDITIONAL LOVE OF GOD

Give thanks to the Lord, for he is good; his love endures forever" (Ps. 118:1). Our view of God shapes our life more profoundly than all else. Spend family devotionals studying God's nature. Study the stories of how God took people who were shy and used them to accomplish great things. Let Moses, Gideon, Jeremiah, David, and Timothy become their heroes. Let them see that God can strengthen them to overcome their fearful tendencies.

Our children need to know that there is a source of love

in their lives that is inexhaustible. They need to see God as a personal, loving Father:

> *The Lord is compassionate and gracious, slow to anger, abounding in love. He will not always accuse, nor will he harbor his anger forever; he does not treat us as our sins deserve or repay us according to our iniquities. For as high as the heavens are above the earth, so great is his love for those who fear him; as far as the east is from the west, so far has he removed our transgressions from us. As a father has compassion on his children, so the Lord has compassion on those who fear him; for he knows how we are formed, he remembers that we are dust. (Ps. 103:8-14)*

Their view of life, themselves, and others will then be shaped by the fact above all facts—"God is love." Upon this foundation can be built a life of confidence. Rooted in this soil, children can draw forth the nourishment and power to become, even in a sinful world, all that God had in mind when he entrusted them to us, their parents.

7

Drug Use and Abuse:
A Lesson on Awareness
Elizabeth Carter Alvarez

There is the story of the young boy who, growing up in a small, predominantly white town, would take the long way around little black boys because he was afraid that if he brushed up against one, the dark color would rub off on him. In discussing the problem of drugs among young people today, it is common for many adults to shy away from the issue for fear of it somehow "rubbing off" on them. "Why should I worry about that?" "My kids are growing up in a Christian home—they wouldn't do drugs." "If my kid were on drugs, I would know it."

All are common attitudes. This avoidance of the reality of the drug problem among American teens today must be dealt with before there can be any solution. Simply looking away from the problem will not make it go away.

The sad fact is that the drug epidemic hits teens of every social class, every city, every religion, every high school, junior high, and even elementary school. One out of eleven high school seniors smokes three and a half marijuana joints a day, and two out of three try drugs before graduation. Although marijuana use has seemed to decline recently, cocaine use has skyrocketed, and alcohol use steadily increases.

Lack of awareness of this rampant problem only contributes to its growth. Paul stated that Satan must not be allowed to outwit us, "For we are not unaware of his schemes" (2 Cor. 2:11). Satan works powerfully to convince people that the drug problem "couldn't happen to us." Any sin, however, can happen to anyone. Peter spoke of Satan prowling around "like a roaring lion looking for someone to devour" (5:8). Unaware Christians are devoured easily, and nowhere is this more true than with the issue of drugs among teens. Paul urged Christians to put on the full armor of God (Eph. 6:8-10). Satan is shooting flaming arrows, and too often, we fling back cotton balls when it comes to combating drug use.

WHAT IS A DRUGGIE?

The term "druggie" usually brings to mind a vivid image of a person with long, stringy hair and a washed-out complexion, peering out of dazed, glassy, bloodshot eyes, with arms full of needle marks, and mumbling incoherently. This image is a real one, and there are many people in this condition. However, "drugginess" begins long before a person reaches this state. A "druggie" is anyone who uses any kind of chemical to deliberately alter his mood. In other words, the star athlete, depressed after a major loss, who goes out to get drunk with the boys to "forget it all" is well on his way to having a drug problem. So is the church-going teen who smokes a few joints to "mellow out" after a fight with his parents.

One might wonder, "Isn't it normal for a kid to try drugs?" It may be normal for an adolescent to drink or smoke one joint out of sheer curiosity or momentary weakness. Any try after the first, however, is not normal. The first try teaches a teen that good feelings can be felt instantly. Any drug used after learning this by experience is a deliberate pursuit of these good feelings. This can so easily start the teen on a cycle of drug use that grows uncontrollably.

DRUGS USED TO COPE EMOTIONALLY

Drugs become a substitute for the emotional coping processes normal people use to deal with life. Adolescence is a time of learning how to deal with extremes—the euphoria of growing up, experiencing first love, responsibility, reaching goals, and the pain of rejection, doubts, poor self-image, and failure. Teens going through these ups and downs not using drugs learn to deal with these in a healthy way—by talking, crying, thinking of solutions, letting time go by, getting back up, and trying again. In other words, these kids grow up.

When drugs come into the picture, the unhealthy coping processes begin. Drugs become an artificial shortcut to whatever mood the teen desires to experience. These adolescents do not learn how to deal with the ups and downs of life and, as a result, they simply don't grow up. Rather than experiencing good feelings from inner accomplishment, positive self-image, and good relationships, the teen gets high. Rather than working through them when the downs come, a drug is used to lift the teen out of the bad feelings. In reality, the bad feelings are never really dealt with, just repressed by the drugs.

Jesus spoke of being "choked by life's worries, riches, and pleasures, and they do not mature" (Luke 8:14). Drugs choke maturity. God wants people to feel sin, but drug users avoid the pain. Their attitude as stated in Isaiah is "Eat, drink, for tomorrow we die" (22:12-13).

People change because they feel bad, guilty, ashamed, or frustrated. "In my distress I called to the Lord" (2 Sam. 22:7). Since drugs take away the bad feelings, they also take away the changes that normally would result if these feelings were felt. Hosea wrote that wine takes away "the understanding of my people" (4:11), and the result of this is ruin (v. 14). Isaiah 5:12, Jeremiah 6:15, and Jeremiah 8:12 all speak of the devastating effect of losing feeling for sin. "They have no shame at all . . . so they will fall among the fallen." Amos put it another way: "You drink wine by the bowlful . . . but you do not grieve over the ruin" (6:6). Habakkuk wrote of the drinker: "Wine betrays him; he is arrogant and never at rest . . . never satisfied" (2:4-5). Change cannot begin to occur until the chemicals are gone and the teen is allowed to feel what he has not let himself feel, and then he can go through the normal, healthy changing process.

FOUR PRINCIPLES

In describing the drug problem, there are four principles that need to be understood. First of all, drug use is a primary condition. The drugs themselves are the cause of motivation, family, and academic problems because they cover up the guilt a normal teen feels when he has done something wrong. As was mentioned previously, until the drugs are eliminated, the teen cannot begin to change.

Second, drug use is progressive. It keeps getting worse. Usually teens begin using alcohol or pot and then progress to pills, hallucinogens, and finally to injecting drugs. The reason for this progression is that as the bad feelings increase, more drugs are needed. Paul wrote about "ever-increasing wickedness" (Rom. 6:19), and about the "continual lust for more" (Eph. 4:19) experienced by people involved in any habitual sin.

The third principle is that drug use is chronic. It keeps cropping up. Many times teens will attempt to get "straight" only to fail time and time again because they have not learned to deal with bad feelings without drugs. Over a period of time, the drugs suppress the will to be self-disciplined about anything. Teens experiencing this failure often feel worthless, thinking, "See, I can't do it." Paul expressed it this way: "I do not understand what I do" (Rom. 7:15). The psalmist spoke of the way sin can flare up over and over again (Ps. 78:9-64).

Finally, drug use is terminal. Not dealt with, its only end is death. The leading causes of death among teens today are accidents, suicide, homicide, and cancer. The first three of these are often related to drug use.

FOUR STAGES

Normally, a teen involved in drugs will go through four easily detectable stages. These are presented below as they appear in the book *Gone Way Down* by Miller Newton, Ph.D.

Stage One of drug abuse is called, *Learning the Mood Swing*. During this stage, the teen learns that chemicals produce "good feelings." The drugs normally used at this time are alcohol and marijuana. The teen discovers that he can feel good quickly and easily and yet not experience negative consequences.

Stage Two, *Seeking the Mood Swing*, is the stage in which the teen begins to actively pursue "getting high." He will plan his drug use and may start skipping school or sneaking out in order to find the time to use drugs. Drug use during this stage normally progresses to inhalants, hash, and pills. During this stage, the dual life begins. The teen will keep his old straight friends while at the same time pursuing his new druggie friendships. Grades often decline during this stage. The teen begins to feel guilty at this stage, and the result is increased drug usage, leading to the third stage.

This third stage is called, *Preoccupation with the Mood Swing*. The teen is literally obsessed with getting high. To avoid the bad feelings he feels when he is off drugs, harder drugs such as mushrooms, PCP, cocaine, LSD, and others are frequently used at this stage. Now straight friends are forgotten, and lying is second nature. The teen begins stealing to support his habit. Family fights occur continually. The teen actually feels distress when not high. Guilt skyrockets along with a feeling of self-worthlessness. The teen experiences his first suicidal thoughts during this stage.

The fourth stage, *Use Drugs to Feel Normal*, is the point at which the teen cannot even function unless he is high. The teen begins to inject drugs during this stage and desperately avoids the extreme pain he feels when he is down. Drugs are used just to feel numb. Being normal now means being high. Physical health disintegrates during this stage. The teen cannot function responsibly in any activity. The teen's identity is gone now, and thoughts of suicide are very frequent.

Several scriptures can give more insight into understanding these four stages. Isaiah spoke of the way people try to hide their sin, which is characteristic of the first stage, Learning the Mood Swing. They "do their work in darkness and think, 'Who sees us? Who will know?' " (29:15). Another typical first stage attitude is found in Isaiah: "Let us drink our fill of beer! And tomorrow will be like today, or even far better" (56:12). In this first stage, teens learn that chemicals make life more fun and few negative consequences are experienced. Isaiah described the second stage, Seeking the Mood Swing. It talks of people who "run after their drinks, who stay up late at night till they are inflamed with wine" (5:11). In Proverbs is a graphic illustration of the third stage, Preoccupation with the Mood Swing: "When will I wake up so I can find another drink?" (23:25-35). By the time a person reaches the fourth stage, Use Drugs to Feel Normal, there is no attempt to hide the problem. "The look on their faces testifies against them: they parade their sin like Sodom; they do not hide it. Woe to them! They have brought disaster upon themselves" (Isa. 3:9).

Drug use is a disaster. Its pattern is one that parents must be aware of in order to fight it.

FACTS ABOUT DRUG USE

1. Alcohol is a drug.

2. A drug problem does not start with the first beer or joint. It potentially begins with white lies, irresponsibility, images (discussed later), and bad feelings such as loneliness, anger, and hurt that are left inside and unresolved. This all can build up and lead to drug use. This behavior during the pre-drug period is often called "dry druggie" behavior.

3. Drugs are used to push down feelings. These feelings,

however, do not go away, so drug use increases.

4. During "dry druggie" behavior, even one's strongest principles and values waver. Any convictions that are simply inherited from the parents will fall as soon as the negative influence on the teen exceeds the positive. This occurs as the pre-drug behavior places the teen around bad influences. This is a very vulnerable time, usually occurring around the ages of eleven to fourteen.

5. Self-opinion is a key factor. Any teen who thinks he has to be like whoever he is around is particularly susceptible to "doing drugs." Most teens have the twisted belief that getting high or drunk gives them more personality. What these teens often lack is appreciation of their own unique personality. Drugs simply mask the natural insecure feelings that need to be dealt with in a healthy way so the teen can grow. The drug-induced personality change lasts only as long as the high, which in itself furthers more drug use.

6. The need for acceptance is another factor that fosters drug use. Drugs draw teens together in a subculture where virtually every member thinks, feels, and acts alike. There is little, if any, individuality, even in the way they dress. This provides a very comfortable environment for insecure teens who feel the need to "fit in." However, like the good feelings, the acceptance lasts only as long as the drugs and druggie behavior last. Again, this furthers more drug use.

7. Certain "images" are signals of drug use, and parents need to be aware of these. Among these are: headbands, feathers hanging from the rearview mirror (which usually have a "roach clip" on the end to hold marijuana joints), punk styles, tight clothing, concert T-shirts, and some flannel shirts. Even teens who are not using drugs but use these "images" are vulnerable because they will draw drug-using teens to them. Other signs to be aware of are: loss of weight, washed-out complexion, red eyes and excessive Visine use, skipping school, talking back to authorities, profanity, stringy hair, slow movements, slurred words, ex-

treme hyperactivity, mood swings, avoidance of family activities, loud behavior, drug-related rock music, poor grades, loss of appetite, depression, acts of violence, changes in friends, lying, vandalism, objects missing from home, dark room, memory loss, sexual activity, leaving drugs and paraphernalia in plain view, running away or threatening to drop out of favorite activities (sports or clubs), neglect of personal hygiene, bruises on skin, persistent cough, dilated pupils, and sneaking out of the house.

8. Curiosity and boredom are also factors. It is easy for teens growing up in a religious environment to feel restless, thinking, "I've got to try something. I can't be the perfect little 'goody goody' forever." The message to get across to these teens is: You are not perfect. You are just as much of a sinner as people who do drugs. They must realize the seriousness of sin—any sin—and understand that any sin they have not fallen into is only by the grace of God.

If teens do see the seriousness of any sin, they will appreciate their salvation and not have to prove how much they need God. Many times teens see people change from rough pasts and respect them. Often, doubts arise such as: "I have not had to change much," and they feel less important than those who have experienced seemingly "greater" changes. What these teens need to realize is that changing from jealousy or laziness are as significant as the change of getting off drugs. Again, sin is sin, and problems are problems. Realizing these principles will help to clear up boredom and curiosity.

PREVENTATIVE SUGGESTIONS FOR PARENTS

After gaining more knowledge about the drug problem, parents will logically wonder, "What can I do to prevent this from happening with my kids?" Parents can do nothing that will completely guarantee that their child will never do drugs, but there are ways to minimize that possibility. Parents' major weapon in fighting drugs is simply awareness—knowing what to look for. When any of the signs that have been mentioned begin showing up in teens, it is not a time to proclaim in denial, "It can't happen to us." It can.

It is not a time to ignore what is going on and hope it will be better in the morning. It won't. It is not a time to withdraw the family into a cocoon that will let no objective outside help penetrate. It is a time to talk, to communicate openly and honestly within the family.

Parents can ask their teens certain questions that will help them be aware of themselves. Teen awareness is equally as important as parent awareness. Teens need to know not just the "horror story" effect of drugs but, more importantly, the attitudes and signs to watch for in themselves that tend to lead to the problem.

The following is a list of questions parents can go over with their teens. Start at a young age. This will help keep communication open and teach both parent and child how to stay in touch with themselves.

1. What do you do with your feelings? When you are hurt, angry, disappointed, or lonely—what do you do? Do you talk about it, or go off into your room and cry by yourself? (Parents, watch this one. It is imperative that teens share what goes on inside them.)

2. How do you feel when you are all by yourself? Empty? Lost? Uncomfortable? Are you calm, serene, happy? (When you are by yourself, that is who you really are.)

3. Do you avoid being by yourself? Do you always have to have the television or radio on?

4. Do you have security in things outside of yourself? How much of your good feelings about yourself are based upon how you look, who your friends are, your boyfriend or girlfriend, or your accomplishments (grades, sports, awards)? Teens need to distinguish between good feelings about the act itself—the home run, the straight-A report card—and the good feelings about the inner quality that made the accomplishment possible. If the good feelings

are only about the act itself, the teen will keep having to "perform" to feel good. If, however, the good feelings are about the inner qualities, such as the perseverance, discipline, and determination that brought about the accomplishment, the teen will form a positive self-image that will keep him going in times of failure. Self-esteem is one of the greatest buffers against the pressures of drugs.

5. Do you always have to be the center of attention? Do you go to extremes to get people to notice you?

6. Do you change your personality based on who you are around? If you do, which one is the real "you"?

7. How much of what you believe is founded simply on what you have been told by others? How much is based on real inner conviction? Do you know why you believe in God, Jesus, the Bible? If not, find out. Inherited beliefs will crumble as soon as the reinforcement is gone.

8. Is it becoming easier to ignore your conscience?

9. Do you "glamorize" other people, thinking, "They have all the fun. I wish I were like ———" If so, why? What is it about these people that you want to be like?

10. How well do you know yourself? What are your good qualities and your weaknesses?

11. How serious do you take sin—any sin?

12. How is your communication with your parents? What would you never tell them? Why not?

These questions are important for any teen to consider, but they are especially helpful in lessening the chance that they will turn to drugs. An adolescent with strong convictions, surrounded with strong positive peer pressure, who knows himself and likes the person he is has a much better chance of saying no to drugs.

Besides the above measures, there are other ways parents can make sure they remain aware of any potential problems. The following is a list of questions for parents to consider and answer honestly.

1. Are you aware of your child's behavior outside home?

Do you visit your child's school, talk to teachers, sports coaches, and other instructors? It is often helpful to "show up" unannounced during the school day, perhaps during gym class to observe your child when he does not know you are watching.

2. When your child gets into trouble—of any kind—do you hide it from the other parent? Many times one parent, usually the mother, is manipulated into "not telling Dad about this one." This is dangerous because when bigger problems arise that stem from the "little ones" that one parent did not know about, that parent is more likely to deny the problem or resent the fact that he or she was left in the dark. Hiding or overlooking problems only feeds the teen's attitude that he is "special" and can get away with virtually anything. Deuteronomy 28:19 and Jeremiah 7:9-11 speak of this attitude: "I will be safe, even though I persist in going my own way." Don't contribute to this mind-set by keeping any misbehavior "safe" from the other parent.

3. Are you easily swayed by your child's words when he is caught doing something wrong? Does your child simply have to say, "I'm sorry," and shed some tears for you to relent and hold back consequences for his behavior? It is important to look at your child's actions, not just his words. Jeremiah 3:4-5 illustrates the way words can be used to manipulate: "Have you not just called to me: 'My father, my friend from my youth, will you always be angry? Will your wrath continue forever?' This is how you talk, but you do all the evil you can."

Make sure your children experience godly sorrow for even the smallest wrongs. This will keep their consciences tender. Second Corinthians 7:8-12 contrasts worldly sorrow with godly sorrow. Worldly sorrow is being sorry for the consequences, not the sin. Godly sorrow produces change. Acts 26:20 states that people must "prove their repentance by their deeds." This is a vital lesson for children to learn early.

4. Do you look through your teen's belongings or room

periodically? This is the way many parents find out about their child's problem—discovering a note mentioning drugs, finding actual drugs or paraphernalia. Be especially aware if your teen leaves his door locked or makes it clear that no one is to enter without permission. Some of this need for "privacy" is typical of every teen, but if this is combined with other behavior mentioned previously, go ahead and search. (And be thorough—it is amazing the creativity teens can exhibit in hiding drugs—such as in stereo speakers, the hemline of drapes, taped behind dressers, in holes in the wall or floor, in pockets of old clothes, behind pictures.) Hebrews 4:12 says, "See to it, brothers, that none of you has a sinful, unbelieving heart that turns away from the living God." See to it! There is nothing wrong with "snooping" when it comes to saving a life.

5. Do you enable your child? Enabling is simply doing for your child what he needs to do for himself. Examples of this are making up their beds, picking up after them constantly, or bailing them out of their irresponsibility. When your child continually forgets his lunch or homework, do you continually bring it to him, thus covering up his mistakes? This constant type of enabling hinders teens from becoming responsible for themselves. When a person does drugs, the drugs "fix" every bad feeling. Don't "fix" everything for your child. Let your child suffer the consequences for irresponsibility—the bad feelings—so he can learn to change. Why should your child change if he knows, "Mom will take care of it for me"? Jeremiah 23:14 states, "They strengthen the hands of evildoers, so that no one turns from his wickedness." How did these people strengthen the hands of evildoers? By "saying to those who follow the stubbornness of their hearts ... No harm will come to you" Parents can unknowingly give this message to their children by never letting them "reap what they sow."

6. What is your reaction when someone reports to you your child's misbehavior? Is your first thought, "No, he

couldn't have done that! There must be a mistake"? Are you open and willing to investigate? Often people outside the family can see what parents do not, and it is wise to always be willing to listen to other's input.

7. How do you verbally communicate with your children? When they have done something wrong, do you simply lecture, or do you share your feelings? Examples of lecturing that usually get nowhere are remarks such as, "Why did you do that?" "I can't believe you would...", or "When will you learn to...?" Contrast the above with sharing actual feelings about your child's behavior: "I am hurt and disappointed that you ..." "It really scares me to know ..." "I am angry that you didn't care enough to ..." This kind of communication is much more likely to get through to your child because he can relate to these feelings.

8. Do you listen to your child? When you ask how your child's day was and you get the answer, "Fine," are you content with that? Do you probe, ask questions, and really find out how his day was? A child is much more likely to open up if he knows he has an interested and understanding listener.

WHEN DRUG ABUSE IS ALREADY OCCURRING

Most of the preceding information is concerned with the awareness and prevention of the drug problem. What about when prevention is too late? In trying to cope with a "druggie" child, insanity can reign in the home. Parents resort to screaming, threatening, and physical force. They often feel guilty, thinking, "What did I do wrong?" The siblings either hide their brother's or sister's problem or fall into the same type of behavior. Everyone in the family becomes a part of the problem.

Usually it takes a major crisis—the teen being kicked out of school, arrested, or overdosing before the parents will finally realize and admit that they have a problem they can no longer deal with on their own. Hopefully, the awareness given in this chapter will help parents see their child's problem before it gets to this point (which is usually the third stage of drug use). If the problem can be caught during the first or second stages, it may be possible to shock the teen out of it by confrontation from Christian peers, elders of the church, and strong discipline measures by the parents.

The problem in dealing with teens farther along in their drug use is that simple confrontation and parental discipline does not remove the drugs or druggie friends from the teen's environment. By the time a person has reached the end of the second and beginning of the third stage of drug use, he is literally preoccupied with getting high. Hosea wrote, "Their deeds do not permit them to return to the Lord. A spirit of prostitution is in their heart" (5:4). The heart itself must be dealt with—the attitudes that led the teen to drugs. But in order to deal with the heart, the drugs, the deeds that "do not permit" him to change, must be eliminated. Recall that as long as drugs are used to change bad feelings, there is no reason for the teen to deal with reality. Therefore, in order for change to occur, the person must be in a drug-free environment.

Here is where many parents balk: "You mean, I've got to put my kid into drug rehab? No way! I'll get him to quit!" And the parents again try to change their child. They move to another town, put the teen in a different school, take him to a counselor or psychiatrist, and yet the teen's behavior worsens because none of these tactics removes drugs from the teen's environment. The pressures pulling the teen farther into drugs are still there and stronger than the parents realize.

These parents must come to grips with the reality and admit, "My child needs more help than I can give." Placing a teen, especially one who has grown up in a Christian home, into a drug treatment center seems harsh and unthinkable to many Christian parents. "Why can't the church help?" they wonder. The fact is that the church can't and God himself won't help a heart unwilling to change. Putting the teen in an environment away from drugs, "druggie friends," and all the false security he has learned to depend on is often the only way his heart can soften so that God's Word can penetrate once again.

What is the biblical principle behind this type of discipline? It is a principle that can be found over and over again in the Bible, and it can be termed "Tough Love." God is the original tough lover. The Israelites were God's chosen people, his treasured possession, his children, and yet he could not control their hearts. "How gladly would I treat you like sons and give you a desirable land.... I thought you would call me 'Father' and not turn away from following me. But like a woman unfaithful to her husband, so you have been unfaithful to me" (Jer. 3:19-20). Time and time again, he would warn them, sending prophets and miracles, and yet time and time again they turned away from him (Ps. 106).

The way God would deal with this was to hand the Israelites over to other nations to humble them (Ezek. 21:24), test them, teach them (2 Chron. 12:7-8), and bring back their feelings for their sin. Second Chronicles 33:10-13 is an example of a very important "tough love" principle: "The Lord spoke to Manasseh and his people, but they paid no attention. So the Lord brought against them the army ... who took Manasseh prisoner, put a hook in his nose, bound him with bronze shackles, and took him to Babylon." God took away all control from Manasseh because of his hard heart. And what was the result? "In his distress he sought the favor of the Lord his God and humbled himself greatly.... Then Manasseh knew that the Lord is God." The principle is this: Sometimes it is necessary to take away control from people in order for them to learn who is in control. Deuteronomy 28:15-68 shows God's attitude toward sin. Always, the purpose of his discipline was to bring about repentance (Deut. 30:1-10).

Some parents might be thinking, "But I've done every-thing for my child!" God can relate to that! Through Isaiah he said, "What more could have been done for my vineyard than I have done for it? When I looked for good grapes, why did it yield only bad?" (5:1-5). Even God wondered why. But he did not just sit around wondering—he took action. The tough love in verses 11-17 was his last resort, and really the only hope in bringing his people back to him. And this type of discipline, this "handing over" of their children to secular programs is often the only hope parents have of saving them from the clutches of drugs.

The Book of Jeremiah is the prophecy of Israel's fall to Babylon because of their sin. They had lost all sensitivity and were intent on rebellion (6:15; 44:16-18). So God handed them over, and Lamentations is the result: confes-sion (1:20), remembering the past and feeling for it (3:19-20), self-examination, and return to God (3:40-41).

The result of God's tough love in Ezekiel 6:8-19 was shame for the past and the realization of God as Lord. Studying Isaiah 9:10–10:20 and portions of chapters 11 and 12 reveal that God's discipline taught true reliance on him (10:20), opened the way for salvation (11:1,10), and brought praise to God (12:1-6).

There are many more examples like these showing the way God would hand over his people to soften their hearts. Again, for parents who think, "I've already done everything," the question is, have you really?

Before discussing how to select treatment programs, there is one other issue to be addressed. Many times parents have the view that, "This is just a stage. He'll grow out of it eventually." This rationale is completely unacceptable biblically. The Bible is clear in its admonition never to tolerate sin.

I will be careful to lead a blameless life—when will you come to me? I will walk in my house with blame-less heart. I will set before my eyes no vile thing. The

*deeds of faithless men I hate; they will not cling to
me. Men of perverse heart shall be far from me; I
will have nothing to do with evil. Whoever ... has
haughty eyes and a proud heart, him will I not endure. No one who practices deceit will dwell in my
house; no one who speaks falsely will stand in my
presence. (Ps. 101:2-7)*

Too often children know that their parents will tolerate
sin, so it is no wonder that the sin continues. Too often
the "stage" that the teen "will surely outgrow" never has
the chance to be outgrown because the teen is killed in
an auto accident or permanently damaged from an over-
dose. Too often, the teen does "grow up"—eventually turning away from the drugs—but the guilt and low self-esteem
are never dealt with. In fighting the sin of drug use, nothing
less than an unwavering, uncompromising head-on attack
will succeed.

To begin with, seek out a family therapist who has experience with drug abuse, then get the entire family into the
initial session, no matter what it takes. It is important to
find a therapist or psychologist who is aware of the sub-
tleties of drug use and is not naive about the previously
mentioned symptoms. If there is a drug problem, an experienced counselor will recognize within three to six sessions
that individual or family therapy before inpatient treatment
is futile. A referral to an inpatient drug treatment program
is then essential. Only after this will outpatient counseling
help.

In selecting a drug treatment program for your child,
there are several criteria a good program will meet. These
will include a drug free environment, peer counseling,
promotion of a drug-free life-style, a cognitive therapy
mode, family treatment, group therapy, and progressive
reintegration.

One such program that meets the above criteria is the
Straight, Inc. program. The program has branches in St.

Petersburg, Florida; Orlando, Florida; Atlanta, Georgia:
Cincinnati, Ohio; and Boston, Massachusetts. This program offers a very beneficial, positive peer pressure type
of environment in which teens are able to take a look at
what drugs have done to their lives. The recovery process
involves "making a commitment to remain free of all mood-
altering chemicals." It involves facing one's past, all those
events that produced guilt, shame, hurt, and pain. Once
the past is faced and cleaned out, the person is then able
to start learning the skills necessary to remain drug free
and to control effectively his or her own thoughts, feelings,
and behavior.

James wrote: "Confess your sins to each other . . . so that
you may be healed" (5:16). Confession is vital for the healing of the soul. Getting out the bad feelings that drugs had
been used to repress is really the only way for the teen to
forgive himself. It is the freeing process that allows the
teen to go on to a productive new life.

Another lesson that Straight teaches its clients is the
lesson of accountability. When a teen enters Straight, he is
told: "You are accountable. It's your fault you're where
you're at, and it's up to you to change." It is extremely
important for the teen to take responsibility for his actions.
As long as there is any denial or blame, the guilt the teen
feels for what he has done cannot be dealt with.

Finally, Straight and similar programs like it realize that
it is not enough to "get the drugs out of the druggie." Old
attitudes, ways of thinking, reacting, communicating, have
to be replaced and renewed. This is illustrated clearly by
Zechariah, who wrote, "Take off his filthy clothes. . . . See,
I have taken away your sin, and I have put rich garments
on you" (3:3-5). After taking off the filthy clothing of drugs,
deceit, guilt, and impurity, the teen must put on the rich
garments of change, honesty, a clean conscience, and godly
relationships. Christ spoke about the consequences of not
going through this "replacing" process:

When an evil spirit comes out of a man, it goes through arid places seeking rest and does not find it. Then it says, "I will return to the house I left." When it arrives, it finds the house unoccupied, swept clean and put in order. Then it goes and takes with it seven other spirits more wicked than itself, and they go in and live there. And the final condition of that man is worse than the first. (Matt. 12:43-45)

The danger in sweeping the past away is that if the teen does not keep putting good back in, he will slip back to former ways and worse. After a teen finishes a drug treatment center, it is vital for him to continue on an upward path of growth. The problem with secular programs is that they have an end. The teen must have a way to keep changing—and here is where Christianity is so important. In the Christian life, there is always room to grow. "Now the Lord is the Spirit, and where the Spirit of the Lord is, there is freedom. And we, with unveiled faces all reflect the Lord's glory, are being transformed into his likeness with ever-increasing glory, which comes from the Lord, who is the Spirit" (2 Cor. 3:17-18).

Christianity is a lifetime transforming process, offering everything the teen thought he would get from drugs—real security, happiness, purpose, and fulfillment.

The drug problem among American youth today is real and a threat to every family. Again, parents' major weapon is awareness, and perhaps even more importantly, the courage to act on that awareness—in prevention and in treatment once prevention is too late. "Finally, be strong in the Lord and in his mighty power. Put on the full armor of God so that you can take your stand against the devil's schemes . . . so that when the day of evil comes, you may be able to stand your ground, and after you have done everything, to stand" (Eph. 6:10-13).

8

Separation and Loss
Kent R. Brand, A.C.S.W.

DESCRIPTION OF THE PROBLEM

The United States has twelve million children who are growing up in single parent families. These children are either products of divorce, the death of a parent, or of a single expectant mother who decides to keep her baby. Other children experience the separation when both of their parents die.

Currently, there are between 300,000 and 500,000 children in the United States who are growing up in foster care or group homes without a permanent family. Some of these children will be reunited with their parents, but others need the permanence of an adoptive home.

No one knows exactly how many adopted children there are in the United States. Most adopted children were placed in their adoptive home as infants; however, a large number of children were placed for adoption from one year of age up to late adolescence.

Whatever the reason for separation, the child very often blames himself. Sometimes he feels, "If only I had been a better person, my parents wouldn't have gotten a divorce," or "I must have done something really bad to have to live in a foster home," and even, "My parents must not like me."

HOW SEPARATION AFFECTS
DIFFERENT AGES OF CHILDREN

Separation affects even the youngest infant to some degree. When an infant goes into foster care or is placed for adoption, there may be a period of time in which the child will withdraw and act despondent. He often is grieving the loss of his parents. This reaction is sometimes referred to as anaclitic depression. He may even resist bonding to the new parents who are ready and willing to give him love and acceptance. Toddlers deal with separation by fantasizing. A child in foster care may say that his daddy is going to come back and get him when the father has actually deserted him permanently. A child whose parents have divorced may fantasize that they will get back together and love each other again.

The most difficult age for a child to deal with separation and loss is between six and twelve. This child has outgrown fantasy and yet is not able to understand separation and loss like an adolescent can. Often this child experiences many psychosomatic and interpersonal problems as well as problems in school. This child will typically turn most of his anger inward toward himself.

If separation occurs while a child is an adolescent, the child may cope by intellectualizing: "Well, Mom and Dad couldn't get along anyway, and it's really for the best that they are getting a divorce." A teenaged child who has experienced frequent separations or even one separation early in life may have a more difficult time in coping with all of the normal struggles of his adolescence.

STAGES OF SEPARATION

Stages following separation include: (1) denial, (2) anger, (3) depression, (4) bargaining, and (5) resolution. The key to helping a child progress through the stages of separation is communication and faith in God.

The first stage of denial is the stage that says, "It can't

be true. Mom and Dad did not get a divorce. I don't believe it."

The next stage is one of anger. "Why did my mom and dad do this to me? I am so upset, so angry." This stage, if not dealt with, could be prolonged for many years.

The natural result of anger is depression. A child may feel there is no use in even trying. School-related, behavioral, psychosomatic, and interpersonal problems often are the result.

The fourth stage is the stage of bargaining, which may be an attempt to bargain with God: "God, if I do this, will you bring back my daddy?" It may be bargaining with another family member or bargaining within the child's mind.

The last stage, resolution, some children may never reach. Resolution occurs when the child accepts the fact that the separation has taken place and will not change. The only way to reach this point with the child is to retrace all the previous steps through detailed communication and by helping the child to develop a trust that God is working the situation out for the best (Rom. 8:28).

COMMUNICATING THE LOSS

The news of the loss should be shared by the adult with whom the child is closest. If the child had a difficult relationship with his parents before the separation, then the separation is going to be harder for him to handle. The child must receive very prompt and specific information about the reasons for the separation. He should be allowed to participate in the family grieving process.

The child needs to know that he is not alone, that God has provided someone to be with him. Truly, God is a God of the fatherless, and he sets the lonely in families (Ps. 68:4-6). At this point, affectionate hugs and touching communicate much more than words can. Ask the child what he has missed about the person he has been separated from in recent times. Encourage the child to talk about the person who is gone. Pictures and special memories can be very helpful in the healing process at this time.

This is crucial time to pray with the child about God's intervention and love for the child. The child should be allowed to ask questions and talk freely about his feelings.

TREATMENT STRATEGIES

> *What do you think? If a man owns a hundred sheep, and one of them wanders away, will he not leave the ninety-nine on the hills and go to look for the one that wandered off? And if he finds it, I tell you the truth, he is happier about that one sheep than about the ninety-nine that did not wander off. In the same way, your Father in heaven is not willing that any of these little ones should be lost. (Matt. 18:12-14)*

Jesus Christ realized that there would be times of separation from the security of being with the family and the ninety-nine. Just as a sheep wanders off and experiences separation from a flock of sheep, so also many children today suffer separation from the significant adults in their lives. Jesus says that each of these children are significant, and he definitely does not want them to perish.

What can we do to help children cope with divorce, death, absence, adoption, and foster care? I believe there are ways to involve ourselves with troubled and even normal children who have experienced loss through a change of school or neighborhood, the loss of health through accident and illness, the loss of a friend, or even the loss of a secret hope or fantasy.

The first strategy in helping children deal with separation is to attempt to reestablish communication with the parents or significant adults, if at all possible. In my early years as a Christian social worker, I was called upon to rescue a five-year-old child, Phil, from a home for the retarded. He was a normal child, but he was acquiring much of the behavior and speech of the retarded. It was indicated that his mother was in favor of giving him up for adoption. After much intense work, I was able to place Phil in a Christian foster home. The next goal was to establish contact with his biological mother to find out her permanent plan for him. I discovered that she wanted Phil to be permanently placed for adoption. I informed her that she not only needed to sign the adoption papers, but she had to come and tell Phil "face to face" about her plans.

I remember that when Phil's mother finally came, he did not act like he was paying attention to her. He was looking around the room and playing with other objects in the room. However, the statement that she would not be his mother anymore, and that he was going to get a new mommy and daddy was deeply imprinted upon his mind. As his social worker, I would see Phil often, and he would ask me if I was going to find him a new mommy and daddy. These frequent questions let me know this child deeply understood the communication that his mother gave to him with her parting words.

Once when Phil was spending the weekend in my home, I offered the evening prayer for the food. Immediately afterwards, Phil abruptly stated, "Mr. Kent, you forgot to pray for me a new mommy and daddy." Eventually, Phil was placed for adoption in a wonderful Christian home. One of the key contributors to the success of this placement was that Phil's mother encouraged him to accept his new parents.

The second message that must be communicated to a child who experiences separation is that God is a God of reconciliation. God did not cause his parents to get a divorce. It was of their own free will. God did not choose death for mankind (Rom. 5:12), but promised that through him, ultimate life and reconciliation could occur (John 10:10). From the very beginning, it was God's intention that families be one. "For this reason a man will leave his father and mother and be united to his wife, and they will become one flesh" (Gen. 2:24). If separation does occur, God desires that reconciliation take place. "All this is from God, who reconciled us to himself through Christ and gave us the ministry of reconciliation: that God was reconciling the world to himself in Christ, not counting men's sins against them. And he has committed to us the message of reconciliation" (2 Cor. 5:18-19).

God has always provided for those who do experience separation and are truly seeking him. In 2 Kings 5, we read of a young girl from Israel who was living in Naaman's household. Since there was no mention of this girl's parents, we can assume that she was separated from them for some reason. The girl's faith in God enabled her to speak out to her master, Naaman, in a very courageous way. "If only my master would see the prophet who is in Samaria! He could cure him of his leprosy."

In Genesis 37, we read of Joseph's separation from his family. This separation took place under malicious and jealous intentions. Joseph could have used this experience as an excuse to become bitter toward life and really hate and distrust people. However, Joseph persevered through extremely difficult circumstances: false accusations, slavery, and prison. Later, when Joseph had an opportunity to avenge his brothers' treatment of him, he forgave them and was reconciled with them.

The separation that Jesus and his disciples experienced from one another was indeed difficult. The key advice that Jesus gave to them in a time of separation would be:

1. "A new command I give you: Love one another. As I have loved you, so you must love one another" (John 13:34).
2. "Do not let your hearts be troubled. Trust in God; trust also in me. In my Father's house are many rooms; if it were not so, I would have told you. I am going there to prepare a place for you" (John 14:1-2).

3. "I am the way and the truth and the life. No one comes to the Father except through me" (John 14:6).

4. "Believe me when I say that I am in the Father and the Father is in me; or at least believe on the evidence of the miracles themselves. I tell you the truth, anyone who has faith in me will do what I have been doing. He will do even greater things than these, because I am going to the Father. And I will do whatever you ask in my name, so that the Son may bring glory to the Father. You may ask me for anything in my name, and I will do it" (John 14:11-14).

5. "If you love me, you will obey what I command" (John 14:15).

6. "I will not leave you as orphans; I will come to you" (John 14:18).

7. "Peace I leave with you; my peace I give you. I do not give to you as the world gives. Do not let your hearts be troubled and do not be afraid" (John 14:27).

8. "Remain in me" (John 15:4).

9. "You will grieve, but your grief will turn to joy. A woman giving birth to a child has pain because her time has come; but when her baby is born she forgets the anguish because of her joy that a child is born into the world. So with you: Now is your time of grief, but I will see you again and you will rejoice, and no one will take away your joy" (John 16:20-22).

10. "I have told you these things, so that in me you may have peace. In this world you will have trouble. But take heart! I have overcome the world" (John 16:33).

Ruth experienced separation from her husband by death (Ruth 1:3-5). However, she used this experience to lead her to a deep and close relationship with her mother-in-law. "But Ruth replied, 'Don't urge me to leave you or to turn back from you. Where you go I will go, and where you stay I will stay. Your people will be my people and your God my God. Where you die I will die, and there I will be buried. May the Lord deal with me, be it ever so severely, if anything but death separates you and me' " (Ruth 1:16-17).

Children who experience separation must begin to move toward establishing a close relationship with someone in their lives.

HELPING A CHILD COME TO A RESOLUTION OF THE SEPARATION

Reasons for separating a child from a parent sometimes involve parental immaturity, neglect, child abuse, alcohol or drug abuse, physical illness, parental rejection, or suicide. It is important to approach the reasons very forthrightly and yet very sensitively and, where possible, using God's Word. A child may feel somehow responsible for the separation, but the adult must assure him that this is not the case. At the same time, empathy for the child's feelings should be shown.

When the child does not have information concerning his personal history, this information needs to be supplied. Claudia Jewett's book, *Helping Children Cope with Separation and Loss,*[1] gives some excellent techniques that will help you in completing this task successfully.

One example would be helping the child complete a "life book." The "life book" is a complete history of the child from infancy to the present. It should include photographs, birth certificates, special mementos (awards, letters from birth parents, and souvenirs), drawings, and a narrative. This enables the child to understand and begin to accept the separation and loss.

Since a child's self-esteem can be damaged through separation and the manner in which separation is handled, it is vital for the concerned adult to pray for wisdom (James 1:5). Repairing a damaged self-esteem requires using all of the suggestions of this book, as well as large amounts of praise, affection, and love. After all, love is the greatest healer in the world (2 Cor. 13:1-8).

CONCLUSION

Since so many children in our society experience separation, it is imperative that concerned adults learn how to effectively help a child go through the separation process. My prayers are that God will grant you success and victory.

Notes

Chapter 2
1. Kevin Leman, *The Birth Order Book* (New York: Dell Publishing Company, Inc., 1985).
2. S. Steinmetz, "Intra-Familial Patterns of Conflict Resolution: Husband/ Wife; Parent/Child; Sibling/Sibling," Dissertation Abstracts International, 36, 8A, (1975): 5586-5587.
3. R. Felsen, "Aggression and Violence between Siblings," *The Social Psychology Quarterly,* No. 46, 4 (1983): 271-285.
4. J. Dunn, "Sibling Relationships in Early Childhood," *Periodical of Child Development,* 54 (1983): 787-91.

Chapter 5
1. James Dobson, *Dr. Dobson Answers Your Questions* (Wheaton, Ill.: Tyndale House, 1983), 75-87.
2. Zig Ziglar, *Raising Positive Kids in a Negative World* (Nashville: Oliver Nelson, 1985), 27-31.

Chapter 8
1. Claudia Jewett, *Helping Children Cope with Separation and Loss* (Boston: The Harvard Common Press, 1982).

Selected Reading

Chapter 1
D. C. Briggs, *Your Child's Self Esteem* (Garden City, N.Y.: Dolphin Books, Doubleday and Company, 1975).
James Dobson, *Hide or Seek* (Old Tappan, N.J.: Fleming H. Revell Company, 1979).
M. Scott Peck, *The Road Less Traveled* (New York: Touchtone Books, Simon and Schuster, Inc., 1978).

Chapter 2
Kevin Leman, *The Birth Order Book* (New York: Dell Publishing Company, Inc., 1985).

Chapter 3
Gordon MacDonald, *The Effective Father* (Wheaton, Ill.: Tyndale House, 1977).
Tim LaHaye, *What Everyone Should Know about Homosexuality* (Wheaton, Ill.: Tyndale House, 1985).
Elizabeth Moberly, *Homosexuality: A New Christian Ethic* (Greenwood, S.C.: Attic Press, 1985).
D. Charles Williams, *The Treatment of Dystonic Homosexuality* (Gainesville, Fl.: MFC Publications, 1985).

Chapter 5
James Dobson, *Dr. Dobson Answers Your Questions* (Wheaton, Ill.: Tyndale House, 1983).
Zig Ziglar, *Raising Positive Kids in a Negative World* (Nashville: Oliver Nelson, 1985).

Chapter 8
Claudia Jewett, *Helping Children Cope with Separation and Loss* (Boston: The Harvard Common Press, 1982).

Appendix

SCHOOL CONTRACT

I, _____, agree to the following this
next week:

_____
problem
_____
problem
_____
problem

Monday

Tuesday

Wednesday

Thursday

Friday

For each day I complete my contract, I will receive the
following number of chips:

1   2   3

1   2   3

1   2   3

To teachers: Please *initial* each day that the above-named
boy/girl has met his/her goal.
Return the contract to the student.

Comments:

Signed: _____
            teacher